Rex Harper moved to Cornwall in 1950, later serving in the RAF as a police dog handler. He worked in a local woollen mill and post office while building up his farm with his wife Julie, becoming the full-time RSPCA warden of the Perranporth centre in 1987.

He was awarded the MBE for services to animal welfare in 2003.

By Rex Harper and available from Headline Review

An Otter on the Aga
An Eagle in the Airing Cupboard

An Eagle
In The
Airing Cupboard

MORE TRUE TALES FROM AN
ANIMAL SANCTUARY

Illustrations by Rex Harper

Rex Harper

headline
review

First published in 2008
by HEADLINE REVIEW
An imprint of Headline Publishing Group

First published in paperback in 2009
by HEADLINE REVIEW
An imprint of Headline Publishing Group

1

Cataloguing in Publication Data is available from the British Library

ISBN 978 0 7553 1803 2

Typeset in Scala by Avon DataSet Ltd, Bidford-on-Avon, Warwickshire

Printed and bound in the UK by CPI Mackays, Chatham ME5 8TD

Headline's policy is to use papers that are natural, renewable and recyclable
products and made from wood grown in sustainable forests. The logging
and manufacturing processes are expected to conform to the environmental
regulations of the country of origin.

HEADLINE PUBLISHING GROUP
An Hachette UK Company
338 Euston Road
London NW1 3BH

www.headline.co.uk
www.hachettelivre.co.uk

*This book is dedicated to all the staff and voluntary helpers
who worked so tirelessly to make a success of the RSPCA
animal welfare centre at Perranporth, in particular
Sue, Karen and Nan. Also Roy and Pat who were always
there for advice and help when it was needed.
Thank you all, it was a privilege to work with you.*

Contents

Acknowledgements

I would like to thank everyone who has helped me recall stories and happenings for this book, often happy memories but some which still tug at the heart strings. Writing about days gone by has put me in touch with old friends and contacts, one of whom is Rose, in whose airing cupboard an eagle found sanctuary, providing me with an interesting title. Thanks also to Garry and George for their support and friendship. A special thank you must go to the RSPCA and their inspectors for the difficult and often upsetting work they carry out. I am proud to have worked with and alongside them.

CHAPTER ONE

Early Birds

I stepped out into the morning gloom to be greeted by the usual chorus of yapping, barking, crowing and cackling animals. As I made my way across the compound and through the gate that separated our house from the catteries, aviaries and assorted pens of the RSPCA centre, the cacophony swelled even louder. I knew all too well why they were getting worked up, but breakfast would have to wait. It was another noise that was preoccupying me right now.

Thanks to the bell we'd fitted on the outside wall of the office a few months earlier, I couldn't fail to hear the telephone ringing. We didn't usually get many calls this early in the day, especially not in January, one of our quietest months. It must be an emergency, I told myself.

Fishing for the keys, I opened up the office, flicked on the light and grabbed the phone behind the reception desk, which was still ringing. Almost immediately a part of me wished I'd ignored it.

'Perranporth RSPCA Centre. Good morn—'

'Ah! About flaming time,' a well-to-do male voice announced. He was clearly disinterested in any pleasantries. 'I've being trying to get hold of you lot all morning but there's been no reply.'

I glanced up at the clock on the wall and saw it wasn't much after 7.30 a.m. 'Well, we don't officially open for a while yet,' I said. 'You should have got the answer machine. Anyhow, what's the problem?'

'I'll tell you what the flaming problem is,' he said. 'There's a bloody great badger in my backyard. It's been there all night and it's wrecking the place. You should see the state of it. It'll cost me hundreds to sort it out.'

I really didn't like his tone. It was as if all of Cornwall's wildlife was my personal responsibility and it was my fault that his garden had an unwanted visitor. But he wasn't the first bad-mannered caller we'd had, and nor would he be the last. I got on with doing my job.

'Right,' I said, looking for my notepad. 'Give me a second and I'll jot down some details.'

By now the first of the centre staff were trickling in, hanging up their coats and getting ready for the day's work. My main assistants, Sue and Karen, were in early as usual. One of the four inspectors who were based in our cramped offices had also arrived, but was already preparing to head out.

It must have been obvious I had a difficult caller on my hands: Karen threw me a look of sympathy before grabbing my mug and using hand signals to ask whether I wanted some tea. I gave her a thumbs-up.

'OK, fire away,' I said to the man on the phone.

The caller gave me an address in Truro. I told him I'd get there as soon as I could, but even this failed to placate him. 'Look. I want it got rid of. Right away. You're supposed to be the animal rescue people, so come down here and do your job and rescue the bloody thing.'

It was pretty obvious that the less said in this particular instance, the better, so I reassured him I would be there by 9 a.m. at the very latest.

'Well, just make sure you're not any longer,' he said, before slamming down the phone.

'Charming,' I muttered to myself.

It was 1989, a dozen or so years since a corner of our farm, Ferndale, a mile or so from Perranporth, on the north Cornish coast, had been taken over by the RSPCA. Until then my wife, Julie, and I had run our own private animal sanctuary, taking in waifs and strays. The RSPCA had transformed our modest little enterprise into the county's only animal welfare centre and an extremely busy, highly professional operation. As warden of the centre, I oversaw a team that included Sue and Karen – two local girls who had proved to be expert all-round animal handlers – Vicky, who was a cat expert, and a stream of voluntary workers, who helped out with exercising the dogs, cleaning cages and feeding the inmates. In addition to the four RSPCA inspectors who used the centre as their base, the county's chief inspector, Les Sutton, also worked out of our offices, so there were times when the building was like Waterloo Station during rush hour, with people playing musical chairs whenever a free seat became available. At this time of year, however, the place was relatively calm.

So far the New Year had been fairly free of drama. During the Christmas and New Year holidays we'd had our usual influx of oiled birds brought in from the coast. A few dozen guillemots and razorbills had been recovered on the beaches, coated in oil from spillages that had lain undisturbed on the seabed until the winter gales had churned them up, causing them to float on the water's surface.

For a few years now we'd had a specialist bird-cleaning centre, equipped with the most up-to-date equipment. By now well practised at dealing with these spillages, our team of bird-cleaners had coped comfortably and a large percentage of the victims had been returned to the sea safe and well.

So with things ticking away quietly, Karen, Sue and I had been able to concentrate on other areas. As usual, we were using January to take stock and prepare for the coming twelve months. There was plenty of paperwork to catch up on, and each year I was required to write an annual report, which I always struggled to finish in time. There were also various repairs that needed doing around the place, and we were developing plans to add a swan compound and a new aviary. The thing that was occupying our minds most, however, was the inspection of the centre that RSPCA headquarters were due to make in February, in just three weeks' time.

The RSPCA were our paymasters and employers. Financially and for support, the centre's existence depended on us getting a clean bill of health from the inspection team they were going to send out. We knew everything had to be shipshape and Bristol fashion in readiness for their arrival, which could come at any time. Their standards were exacting, and rightly so. As a consequence, the girls and myself were working hard to get things in order. We'd even drawn up a timetable for working our way around the compound carrying out the various repairs that were required. I'd hoped to tackle one of the catteries myself this morning, but my early caller had put paid to those plans.

'Where are you off to looking so miserable?' my wife, Julie, asked, as I emerged from the office and headed towards the van. Dressed in a thick jumper and wellington boots, she had just finished tending to the collection of goats, sheep and cattle we kept in the few acres of grazing land that we'd acquired with the farm.

'Truro. To catch a badger,' I said.

'Hope he doesn't bite,' she said, smiling.

'I'm not too worried about the badger. It's the grumpy so-and-so who called in about it who's bothering me. He bit my head off just for letting the phone ring for a couple of minutes.'

This was half true at least: I really wasn't worried about retrieving the badger. I'd been called out to deal with my fair share of them over the years. They were never easy creatures to placate and always had to be treated with caution. I knew of one trainee vet who'd come off second best dealing with a badger. He'd come over to the centre to see one that had been found injured in nearby sand dunes. Despite warnings from Julie, he had tried to pick up the apparently sleeping animal from its basket. The badger had snapped out of its false slumber and bitten the chap's hand really badly. There had been blood everywhere and the vet had had to have stitches. I knew the key was to use the right equipment. So, having gulped down the mug of tea that Karen had brought out to me, I loaded the van with a grasper – an adjustable noose on a long pole – thick gloves and a carrying basket.

I arrived in Truro well before 9 a.m., as promised, though I soon realised I would get no thanks for keeping my word. The property turned out to be a large town house near the middle of the city. No sooner had I pulled up than I was met at the front gate by a tall, red-faced man dressed in an immaculate suit. Predictably, he wasn't even prepared to grunt a good morning. Instead, rather like a member of the landed gentry dispatching a delivery boy to the tradesman's entrance, he dismissively pointed me towards a gate at the side of the house.

'It's back there, in the yard at the rear of the house,' he said. 'And do try not to make any more mess while you're in there.'

'I'll try,' I said through gritted teeth.

The man disappeared back into the house, and I ventured down the alley leading to the rear. The backyard was surrounded by a high wall, above which there was thickly hedged land. At first there was no obvious sign of a badger, although its handiwork was plain to see. I guessed that the badger must have fallen into the yard from the hedge above and found itself trapped in the enclosed garden. Panic-stricken, it had torn chunks of wood from the bottom of the garden gate, then rampaged around the yard, scattering a large pile of firewood and flattening some raised flower beds. I couldn't help smiling at the carnage the badger had caused. It wasn't physically possible to make any more mess, I thought. A small voice inside me was saying, 'Couldn't have happened to a nicer chap.'

Scanning the scene, I soon discovered where the intruder had ended up. Its trail of destruction led to a bale of peat. Peering inside the bale, I could see the distinctive black and white markings of the badger, which was curled up in a ball, pretending to be asleep. It was my responsibility to remove the badger before it did any more damage to the premises or itself, so, setting down the carrying basket, I started to ease the grasper into the peat bale towards the inanimate shape curled up inside it.

As the unfortunate trainee vet had discovered for himself, badgers often make out that they're asleep. They use the technique as a defence mechanism, a last resort when they're cornered. I wasn't fooled, though. I knew only too well that the wily creature was really sizing up the situation. It would, in all likelihood, uncurl like lightning and attack if touched, so I moved in carefully.

Sure enough, at the first touch of the grasper's noose on its neck the badger lifted its head ready to snap. It did so just sufficiently for me to work the noose over its neck.

'Got you,' I said, relieved.

The job was far from complete, however. My next task was to lift the badger into the carrying basket – no easy feat. Understandably, the badger really didn't like being ensnared like this and started snarling viciously. Badgers aren't small creatures. They can grow to forty-five pounds, or twenty kilograms, in weight. This one wasn't far off that size, and as it started thrashing around, I found it a real effort to contain it. The danger now was that the grasper could strangle the badger, so I had to move fast. Fortunately, I had the carrying basket ready. I rapidly manhandled the struggling creature inside and strapped the lid down while it pushed its snout against the wire, gamely trying to escape.

I was breathing rather heavily when I emerged from the alleyway leading to the front of the house. As I struggled to carry the basket towards the van, one or two passers-by stopped to see what all the fuss was about. A couple of young children were particularly fascinated by the captive creature.

'Careful – he bites,' I had to caution them when they got a little too close to the basket.

To the owner of the house, however, the animal held no fascination whatsoever. The lord of the manor emerged with his briefcase and umbrella and a newspaper under his arm. 'At last,' he said. 'If your people answered their phone at a reasonable time, we could have sorted this situation out hours ago. Now I'm late for the bloody office,' he added, striding past me and waving his umbrella like a rapier.

After carefully placing the badger in the back of the

van, I returned to close the garden gate. As I did so, I couldn't help but notice a stream of rather unpleasant-looking brown slime leading all the way along the garden path and nearly up to the front door of the house. The badger's capture had clearly had a detrimental effect on its bowels, which had opened uncontrollably. The resulting mess had dripped through the wire mesh at the bottom of the cage, thankfully missing my trousers but streaking the path in the gross-smelling liquid. For a moment I considered clearing it up but then thought better of it. I made a mental note to make sure the office phone was on answer machine that evening.

Surveying the local landscape, I spotted a lane that led to an area of grass- and scrubland. This seemed a good place to let the badger go. It would be well acquainted with this kind of terrain, I felt sure. I drove the van as far as I could, then hauled the basket out and on to the ground. As I'd hoped, the moment I opened the gate on the carrying basket the badger shot off into the bushes without so much as a backward glance. At least I have one satisfied customer this morning, I thought to myself.

The Cornish weather is always unpredictable during the early months of the year. As I headed back to the centre in the van after freeing the badger, I saw that the blue skies were being consumed by banks of swirling grey clouds that were being driven in from the coast. I didn't like the look of them at all. Sure enough, within a few minutes the first waves of rain were lashing down against my windscreen. From the way the trees were bending and twisting in the fields and the van was being buffeted around on the road, it was clear the winds were building in force. By the time I had reached home, they were strong enough to wrench the van's door from my grasp as I climbed out. Out at sea, conditions would be terrible. The turbulence would be churning up more old oil on the seabed. It wouldn't be long before we'd be getting our first oil-soaked casualties. I knew this would mean a busy few days ahead.

Shielding my face from the lashing wind, I ran across the compound to the office. There hadn't been any reports of oiled birds – yet. But there would be, I was certain. The girls told me it had been fairly quiet that morning. A family had dropped in on the off chance we had a dog that might make a pet. In years gone by, people often walked away with a new companion there and then. That had changed, however. We had seen far too many dogs returned to us within days of having left. Now we had a policy of vetting potential owners carefully via home visits and detailed questionnaires, so Sue had taken the family's details and told them we'd be in touch.

The girls then told me that there had been a couple of reports of sightings of stray dogs. A lady had also reported a horse she believed was malnourished and being poorly cared for by its farmer owner. All had been referred to the inspectors, whose job it would be to check them out. The only significant arrivals that morning had been two feral cats, which one of the inspectors had caught at a building site near Newquay. Karen and Sue had taken them to the small isolation unit where feline newcomers spent their first week with us while they were vaccinated, checked over for parasites and assessed for temperament.

I had a meeting at the RSPCA's regional headquarters in Exeter later in the day and wasn't going to be around during the afternoon, so I had a quick look at the two cats before heading back home to change into something that didn't smell of badger. They were a scruffy pair, half-grown tabbies with wild eyes and unkempt fur. Thin and obviously hungry, the two cats had settled down in a cage in the isolation unit and were already making short work of a plate of food. They seemed content enough, and there were no obvious signs of serious problems. With the weather looking more menacing by the second, I was more concerned about the imminent bird arrivals and didn't dwell on the cats for more than a couple of minutes.

The meeting and the long cross-country drive to Exeter and back took up most of the afternoon and early evening. The weather was, if anything, getting worse. Crossing Bodmin Moor, the winds had been so wild that dead branches and twigs had been flying dangerously across the road in front of me. As I pulled into the relative shelter of Ferndale, the gale was still driving in from the coast, bringing with it squalls of dense, sheeting rain. The sky looked as grey as slate, and tuning in to the shipping forecast, there were warnings of more storms to come in the days ahead. The outlook was grim in the extreme.

To no one's surprise, the first bird casualty had arrived mid-afternoon when a man from nearby Perranporth had arrived with a gannet wrapped in a large towel. He'd found the bird on the beach with large quantities of oil on its back and wings. It was the first of what had turned into a stream of avian casualties. Soon afterwards another gannet, four guillemots and a razorbill were brought in. To judge by the phone calls we'd received, there were many more to come. I knew already that we would have to call in our volunteer bird-cleaners for the days that lay ahead.

I spent a little time that evening inspecting this first wave of birds. You can tell a great deal from the weight and fitness of an oiled bird, in particular whether it came into contact with the oil close to shore or further out to sea.

Some seabirds only come ashore during the breeding season, when they find nesting sites on the ledges of tall cliffs or the tops of rocky islands, so a bird's normal reaction when it gets oil on its plumage is to stay at sea for as long as possible, even though the oil prevents them from diving and catching fish as normal. The bird will remain out at sea until it is too weak to fight the pull of the tide any longer and is eventually washed ashore. If the oiling takes place a long way out at sea, many birds may not arrive on the shore until it is too late. Those that do make it may be badly dehydrated and weak after going for days without food. On the other hand, if the oil was close to the coast, the affected birds may come ashore far quicker and so will stand a much better chance of survival.

Inspecting these birds, I got the clear feeling that most had been oiled close to shore. They were in relatively good physical condition. Each of the new arrivals had been treated the same way by the girls. They had been placed in indoor pens and medicated so as to push any ingested oil through their gut. They had then been left to feed and rest for a day before we started the long process of cleaning. One or two of the birds looked a little weaker than the others, but with a day's rest and some food I felt fairly sure they had a good chance of pulling through.

Mildly comforted by the condition of the birds, I decided to check on the two tabbies in the isolation unit. It had been such a hectic day I hadn't looked at them as closely as I might have done. I'd left it to Karen and Sue to begin their treatment. As I held the smaller of the two cats up to the light, however, I saw something that bothered me a little. Although at first glance it looked well enough, there was a small drop of grey mucus in the corner of one of the cat's eyes.

When cats are in poor condition, runny eyes are not uncommon, but they can also be the first symptoms of something worse, in particular viruses such as cat flu. And that was the last thing I wanted at the centre. The cat-flu virus can be pretty lethal when it occurs in a cattery. Every cat has to be put under the charge of a vet, who administers antibiotic injections and advises on individual cases. All adoptions stop, and no fresh cats can be admitted until the vet has given the all-clear, which can mean a wait of several weeks until things return to normal.

In the thirty or so years since Julie and I had started taking in animals, we'd managed to avoid it, but we'd seen its impact elsewhere and knew how lucky we'd been to be spared. With the centre inspection imminent, it would be disastrous if it struck us now. The last thing we needed was a cattery in quarantine and a centre full of sickly cats.

We'll have to keep a careful eye on those two, I told myself, suddenly rather alarmed at the turn of events that had befallen us over the last twenty-four hours.

As I left the cattery, then switched off the lights in the office, I heard rain beginning to hammer on the roof. Stepping outside into the porch, I could hear the wind howling. This was going to be a rough night.

So that people could leave birds with us at any time, we always kept a portable emergency cage in the centre's porch. Checking it now, I found another three guillemots had been placed there. They would have to be taken to the unit, ready to be dealt with in the morning, so I picked up the cage and stepped out from the shelter of the building back into the compound. As I did so, a sudden squall hit me, dispensing with it what felt like half a bucket of rainwater. I was soaked to the skin. It never rains but it pours, I thought to myself.

CHAPTER TWO

Weathering the Storm

As I had suspected, the storm that night was severe and particularly savage out at sea. Listening to the weather forecasts on Radio Cornwall early the next morning, there was talk of tankers coming close to running aground. To no one's surprise, by midday we had taken collection of almost a hundred oiled birds. It had turned into a major incident. I couldn't help shaking my head philosophically. As so often happens in life, just when you think things are drifting along quietly, disaster strikes.

Fortunately, we had become well drilled in dealing with situations like this. Early that morning, Nan, who led our team of volunteer bird-cleaners, had, in her usual quiet, efficient way, contacted her colleagues. All dressed in overalls and plastic aprons, they were in the bird-cleaning unit already, preparing the bowls and sinks ready to make a start treating the birds.

In most cases, oiled birds need two washes. The first wash involves the bird being placed in a bowl of warm water and working washing-up liquid into its plumage. The liquid emulsifies the oil and before long the natural colour of the bird's plumage is visible. After about twenty minutes, the bird is taken out of the bowl and rinsed with a warm-water spray, before being placed in a large pen with an infrared lamp suspended overhead. It is then free to preen its feathers and dry out. At this stage there is invariably some oil, and quite a bit of soap, left in the bird's plumage. The second, and with luck the final, wash takes place two days after the first so as to allow the bird time to rest and recover from the stress of being handled.

When I left the unit, Nan and her team were immersing the first birds in water.

As the day wore on, the clean-up operation kept everyone pretty busy. The cleaning bays in the unit accumulated a lot of droppings and mess during the washing process. It was important that conditions were as clean and hygienic as possible for both birds and humans, so as the specialist cleaners got on with their work, the rest of us pitched in by regularly scrubbing down dirty areas.

The influx of birds was now placing a huge strain on the centre. As well as the cleaning operation, there was the birds' food supply to maintain – no easy task. We were getting in a wide variety of seabirds, each of which required a particular diet. For instance, the smaller birds, like the guillemots and razorbills, required a constant supply of sprats, while the gannets would eat only medium-sized mackerel. Seabirds like puffins were fed on sand eels, while frozen plankton was kept on hand in case there were any really tiny birds, such as storm, or Leach's, petrels, among the casualties.

Our local fish supplier was based at the village of Chapel Porth, four miles from the centre, and that afternoon I made the first of what I felt sure was going to be a regular series of trips to collect boxes of freshly frozen fish. By the time I'd returned and filled the centre's large deep-freeze, the day seemed to have gone in a flash.

I had been so busy dealing with the incoming birds I had almost forgotten the cat with the eye discharge. When I finally found myself a few minutes to check the isolation unit, there was good news and bad. On the positive side, the cat, although pretty scrawny and unhappy at being caged, seemed no worse. Its eye discharge had not deteriorated, but neither had it got any better, so the dreadful prospect of flu hadn't dissipated. And with so much going on at the centre, I knew it would be all too easy for someone or something to spread it from these two cats to other parts of the centre.

The consequences were too grim to contemplate. So just to make certain that any possible infection was not spread, I let the rest of the staff know that I was placing the isolation unit out of bounds to everyone but me. From now on I would take over the cleaning and feeding of the cats myself.

'Better to be safe than sorry,' I told everyone.

*

The next day began on a more depressing note still. The weather was looking even less promising, with banks of solid, rain-freighted clouds massed up overhead. Fortunately, however, the cleaning team were now working like – excuse the pun – a well-oiled machine. The first batch of birds were recovering well from the initial cleaning and would soon be ready for their second wash, while the new arrivals were being processed quickly, efficiently and with – in the main – positive results.

This morning, with everything under control in the cleaning unit, I wasted no time in heading out to see the sickly cat. To my consternation, I found that the cat's other eye was now discharging mucus. Not a good development. Fortunately, I saw that the cat's temperature was a normal 101.4 degrees. Its appetite was still healthy enough and it was clearing its food dish. Its motions appeared normal, but something was obviously not right. Hard as I tried to be positive, at the back of my mind I still suspected cat flu. Back in the office, I decided to ring the centre's regular on-call vet, Mike, and ask him to come and give me a second opinion.

One of the first signs of cat flu is a loss of interest in food. This happens because the mucus that is accumulating in the cat's nostrils inhibits its sense of smell. But this was certainly not the case with our cat. It was still eating heartily. The vet was puzzled. He checked the cat's temperature, as I had done, and looked it over thoroughly, but nothing obvious came to light. After giving a vitamin injection, he left, telling me to keep a close watch and to inform him of future developments.

'Don't worry, Rex,' he told me. 'I'm certain it won't be flu.'

I wasn't so sure.

I spent the rest of the day doing all I could to support the bird-cleaning team, who were now dealing with close to two hundred birds in all. Some of the earliest arrivals were now ready for their second wash, and the team of helpers were making the final preparations to begin the job. Bowls were scoured, the floors of the bird pens were laid with fresh paper and towels, and the shower sprays were tested to ensure that the water was the correct temperature. This was by far the more important of the two washes and required much skill and care. If everything was done correctly, the birds would then be completely clean and waterproof. With luck they would be able to return to the sea within just a few days.

I watched as Nan and her team got to work. The process began with a quick wash in warm water, during which the washers looked out for any remaining oil on the birds' plumage, working in washing-up liquid to remove it if necessary. Each bird was then placed on an upturned washing-up bowl covered with a towel, where it had its plumage sprayed with warm water. This again was a painstaking process. Each and every feather had to be lifted so as to be sprayed and washed clean of any soap.

As this process went on, the washers got a good idea of how well the cleaning operation had gone on each bird. At this point, tiny drops of water could be seen collecting on the feathers. This was where the water was being repelled by the natural oil in the feathers. This was called 'beading' and was a good sign that all was going well, that the spray was in fact waterproofing the bird.

It was slow work. The spraying process can take twenty minutes or more. Once each bird was deemed fully waterproof, it was placed in a large indoor pen lined with clean paper and towels. It would remain there until the following day, when the cleaners' work would be put to the test and the bird would be placed on the testing ponds to ensure that it was completely waterproof. This was always a time to hold one's breath and hope.

By late afternoon the cleaners had given dozens of birds a second wash. They headed home for a well-deserved rest. As silence descended over the centre, I did my evening rounds, finishing up in the isolation unit. The two feral cats were together in their cage but now one looked a lot brighter than its companion. Its coat was becoming sleek and it appeared to have grown since its arrival.

Unfortunately, the other one still looked pathetic, with its weeping eyes and lacklustre coat, and as I spent a moment observing it, things got even worse. Suddenly the sick one got up and walked to the corner of its cage where it promptly started to vomit, almost falling over with the effort. My heart sank. That's it, I thought. We've got cat flu for certain. Feeling rather dejected, I fetched some detergent and cleaning cloths to clear up the mess. My mood was soon changing, however. It isn't often that cleaning up animal mess lifts my spirits, but on this occasion it did. Within the yellowy vomit I could make out some distinctive tubular shapes moving around. Worms.

Cats were automatically wormed on arrival at the centre, and these two had been no exception. I checked again and there was a tick against 'worming' on the information card clipped to the outside of the cats' cage. The girls had done their job, as I'd expected. But sometimes a cat would, unbeknown to us, regurgitate the worming tablet and this is what must have happened here. My guess was that this cat had been heavily infested and was still carrying a large number of the parasites. No wonder the animal had continued to lose condition. Suddenly I saw some hope. If this had been the cause of the runny eyes and general poor health, a further worming might do the trick. I wasted no time in administering one. This time I made certain that the worming tablet was well and truly swallowed. After inserting the tablet in the cat's throat, I held its mouth closed for a short time until I was satisfied it had gone down.

Would this be the turning point for the little cat and the end of our worry about infection? Only time would tell. For the first time in days, however, I felt quietly confident.

*

When I stuck my head in the cattery the following morning, the signs were still good. There was no further evidence of vomiting in the cats' cage, and although the sickly tabby did not appear any different, it had eaten its dish of food and, as I watched it for a moment, even attempted a half-hearted licking of its paws before curling up with its companion and going to sleep.

Early days, I told myself. It would take some time before the benefit of the freedom from the worms took effect, but at least things seemed now to be heading in the right direction.

A corner seemed to have been turned in the cleaning unit too. To gauge whether a bird is ready to return to the wild, we let it bathe and splash around in our testing ponds, fibreglass constructions containing eighteen inches or so of water. If the cleaning process has been successful, the bird's plumage will repel the water. If it hasn't worked, damp patches will be visible on its feathers and another wash may be necessary.

Of the twenty guillemots and razorbills bobbing about on the pond this morning, sixteen had proved themselves to be fit for release. After a couple of days' rest, the four failures would be returned to the cleaning room for a further wash, then taken back to the pond. The bird-washing team were delighted with their results. It is a great feeling when one sees a bird returned to its original beauty that days earlier had been little more than a blob of oil. And it is an even better feeling to know that you have been responsible for the revival in its fortunes.

There was still a way to go, but things were progressing well. It wouldn't be long before that exhilarating moment when the birds would be released from the Cornish clifftops to resume their life out on the Atlantic Ocean. Perhaps, a little like our birds, we had weathered our own particular storm.

CHAPTER THREE
Parting Company

The early morning sun was still low in the sky, but the last of the sea mists was already clearing. Below us, the Atlantic stretched into the distance, a seemingly endless expanse of shimmering grey and green.

'Couldn't be better. Let's get them out and on their way,' I said.

With Nan and two other volunteers from the cleaning unit, I'd set off at first light and driven up to our regular bird-release site, on the cliffs between the village of St Agnes and the smaller holiday resort of Porthtowan. Inside the vehicle were half a dozen cages full of cleaned seabirds, now ready to return to the wild.

I always tried to involve some of the bird-cleaners when birds were being released. Seeing the birds flying away fully restored like this was the gilt on the gingerbread for them. I had also learned to come out either early in the morning or late in the evening, when the coast's large population of gulls were less active. As the daylight grew stronger, they would be out in force, preying on anything that looked small or was behaving abnormally, as these newly released birds would.

I am an early riser anyway, but even if I weren't, I would never have regarded it as a hardship to come out here while most of the rest of the world was asleep. To me, it is one of the most breathtakingly beautiful spots on the whole north Cornish coast. The towering cliffs, their tops covered with a carpet of wild flowers in spring and summer, look out over a spectacular seascape. To the north, the three miles of Perranporth Beach stretch away into the hazy distance. To the south-west, half a mile from shore, the Bowden Rocks, known locally as the Cow and Calf, rise from the sea, surrounded by white flocks of kittiwakes, whose calls can be heard faintly even from a distance.

Each of us took a cage and headed down the mossy slope towards one of the best release spots, on some large boulders with flattened tops that had formed a natural rock garden a hundred feet above the sea. Once there, we began preparing the birds for their release back into the wild.

Experience had taught me that birds respond to their newfound freedom in very different ways. Some are in such a hurry to leave they run across the rocks and are flying away on whirring wings almost as soon as you let them loose. Others, however, assess things more carefully and stay on terra firma for a while before reaching the decision to fly away. Gannets, in particular, are careful birds and always take their time, weighing up the wind currents before stretching their huge wings and calmly soaring away over the waves. This morning's batch of birds proved as diverse in this respect as ever. While the guillemots wasted little time in floating upwards and away from the land, the gannets took a moment to compose themselves before flexing their wings.

Not all birds were suited to these early morning releases. Manx shearwaters, for instance, are semi-nocturnal birds and are much safer when released at dusk, when the risk of predators is low. I would return later that evening, probably with Julie, to release a couple of them that we'd been treating.

If I'm honest, evening was always my favourite time on the cliffs. Julie would often come with me, and together we would sit and watch the sun disappearing into the sea, marvelling at the beauty of our surroundings, a haven of peace in a noisy, frantic world.

That morning it took the three of us ten minutes or so to release all the birds from the baskets. Chatting together as we worked, each of us was happy with the way things had gone over the past two weeks. As usual, we'd lost a few birds, most of them because they'd ingested too much oil, but the bulk of our patients had responded well to the cleaning process and had made it back into the wild safely.

Nan and her team must have been looking forward to a well-deserved lie-in, but as they watched the birds disappear into the wide blue yonder, all seemed pleased to be here at this ungodly hour.

'Until the next time,' one of them said, waving goodbye as the last of the birds headed out to sea.

On arriving back at the centre around mid-morning, I recognised the old, rather battered estate car pulling up outside the entrance gates. It belonged to an elderly lady who bred German shepherds a few miles away, on the other side of St Agnes. I found her in the office, in conversation with Karen.

'Morning, Mr Harper,' she said. 'Busy as usual, I see.'

'No peace for the wicked,' I said.

'That's true enough.'

'Anyhow, what brings you over today?'

'I was just explaining to your lady here, I've got a black and tan bitch that needs rehoming.'

'I see.'

'Any chance you could take her in? She's in the back of the car.'

I have never been too happy about the way breeders dispose of their dogs once they are no longer of commercial value, but at least in this case the breeder was asking us for help, and not simply disposing of the dog indiscriminately. I invited the lady to take a chair and asked her the usual list of questions: has the dog been used to family life? Is she safe around children? Is she house-trained? Is she good-natured?

'Oh, yes,' she replied to all of my questions.

'Well, if she's as good a dog as you say she is, we shouldn't have any problem placing her in a good home,' I said. Deep down, however, I wasn't so sure. At the back of my mind, there were other questions bubbling away. I couldn't help wondering why she had come to us, why the dog hadn't been sold. I had no evidence to suggest that there was a problem. Far from it – to all intents and purposes the dog seemed friendly and was a good-looking specimen. I pushed my doubts to the back of my mind and told the woman to leave the dog with us.

The dog that jumped out of the back of the lady's car was called Rea. She was attractive-looking, relatively well kept and healthy in appearance. She looked friendly too and, when I placed her in the kennels, seemed to get on well with the other dogs.

That evening Julie and I took all our dogs out into the fields as usual for some exercise. Rea joined in willingly and seemed to enjoy running loose, fetching sticks and chasing rabbits.

'What do you think?' I asked Karen, who had always had a good eye for dogs.

'She seems fine,' she said. 'Can't see any major problems.'

'Perhaps I misjudged you,' I said to Rea that night as I locked up the centre.

But of course I hadn't. I'd learned a long time ago to trust my feelings, but for some reason this time I overrode them. I would soon regret doing so.

A couple of evenings later, as the dogs ran loose once more in the fields, I noticed Rea standing staring into space. I called her name several times, but she didn't respond. I decided to approach her and put on her lead.

As I walked towards her, she turned her head, showed her teeth in a snarl and, after spinning round, galloped off across the field and into the wood. I was taken completely by surprise. I'd never seen this kind of behaviour in a German shepherd before. I set off in pursuit, running into the wood and calling Rea's name, but it failed to bring her back. I pressed on a little and after a minute or two, through the trees, down a further field and across the stream, I could see Rea running around in a neighbour's garden. Unfortunately, by the time I had crossed the stream and reached the garden, Rea had disappeared.

This isn't a healthy situation, I told myself. I headed back to the centre and jumped in the van. I couldn't have a dog that was supposedly under my care running loose. I drove around the roads and lanes, looking in every field and gateway, but there was no sign of her.

In the late 1980s, before the advent of dog wardens, I worked closely with the local police where stray dogs were concerned, so the following morning I contacted the local police station.

'Is it dangerous?' the duty constable asked, after I'd given him a description of the dog.

He caught me out with this question. It was something I hadn't considered. Up until the previous evening Rea had been an amenable and friendly dog, but the memory of her standing snarling at me could certainly not be ignored. I had to be honest, so I explained the situation to the constable in as much detail as possible.

After a moment's thought we decided that the best course of action was to ask Radio Cornwall to broadcast a description of Rea. We were on good terms with the station and they immediately agreed, emphasising that anyone who saw the dog should phone me or the police. Under no circumstances were they to try to corner or restrain the animal themselves. Rea was too much of a loose cannon for that, we agreed.

Two days later I received a call from a man who lived a mile or so away. 'There's a dog standing in the road outside my house,' he said. 'Sounds like the German shepherd that's gone missing from your place.'

His description certainly seemed to fit, and sure enough, ten minutes later I climbed out of the van to find Rea standing in the road. She had the same vacant look in her eyes as she had when I had approached her in the field two evenings before. There was no doubt in my mind that she recognised me. When I called her name, she walked a few steps towards me. Great, I thought, and opened the rear door of the van to allow her to jump in. Just as she was approaching the back of the van, however, she stopped suddenly, turned and shot off down the road, turning eventually into an open gate.

I don't understand this, I said to myself, genuinely baffled by her behaviour. It couldn't have been the prospect of riding in the van that had scared her: she had ridden in the van quite happily on several occasions and had never seemed the slightest worried. What could her problem be? Was it the centre? The other dogs and animals there? Was it me, or was it something in her past? This was one of the perennial frustrations with dogs that were rescued or handed over by people without any real explanation – you never knew what sort of existence they had had before arriving with us. And so it was with Rea. I really had no clue what was wrong with her.

I headed in the direction of the gate through which she had disappeared, but when I walked into the open field, there was no sign of her. Once again she had vanished without trace. This was a situation that I could well have done without. Not only did I have one of the centre's dogs running loose, but here was an animal that, due to her sudden change of character, could well become dangerous if she were cornered. I was now genuinely worried that someone could get badly bitten. I was also concerned for Rea herself. What was she going to do for food? Was she going to rummage in rubbish bins, or, heaven forbid, was she going to attack the sheep that were so plentiful in the area and get herself shot in the process? In both instances, the consequences for the RSPCA – and me – could be catastrophic. If either of these things happened, there would be legal action. That would be embarrassing for the RSPCA and might well put my position as the centre's warden on the line. It didn't bear thinking about.

I had long experience handling German shepherds. As a young man in the RAF, I had been responsible for training several of them, and I'd taken in a dozen or more since Julie and I had started an animal sanctuary at the end of the 1950s. They were among my favourite breeds of dog. In general, they were not the type of dog to run off for seemingly no reason, although it could happen, as I knew from experience.

Rea reminded me of another German shepherd, called Sabre, who spent a few weeks with us while we tried to find him a good home. Sabre had had a bad start in life. He was the product of an impulse buy on the part of his owner, who had liked the idea of being seen with a large dog but had no knowledge of how to train one or look after its general welfare. When Sabre became difficult and unruly at about eighteen months of age, the disillusioned owner brought him to the centre and signed him over to our care, walking away without a second glance at the dog. Hardly surprisingly, Sabre was extremely rough around the edges. He had very few manners and even less experience of life in general, but he was bright and quickly learned basic obedience.

German shepherds are highly intelligent dogs and like being spoken to. Sabre was no exception and he and I quickly established a bond. Unfortunately, he became so attached to me that he wanted to be with me all the time. This would have been great if he was going to remain my constant companion, but he wasn't – he was going to be moved to a new home. Predictably, this caused problems when potential owners visited.

When one young man arrived with the intention of adopting Sabre, I was delighted because he already had a German shepherd and lived at a coastal village six miles away, where there was plenty of space for exercising dogs.

It seemed an ideal place for our troubled dog to enjoy life at last.

The initial meeting went well, so, following a home check, Sabre moved to his new home, where we were pleased to see he seemed compatible with the other dog. As a precautionary measure, I warned the new owner to be careful for the first few days in case Sabre tried to run off. The owner agreed to keep him on a lead on walks, but allowed him to run loose in his back garden, which was surrounded by a six-foot wall.

Two days after he'd taken in Sabre, however, the owner rang me in a frantic state to tell me that the dog had jumped the back wall and vanished into the vegetation along the nearby cliffs. The distraught owner had walked for hours calling the dog but to no avail. Frustratingly, he had spotted him briefly in a disused quarry, but Sabre had vanished once again into the thick gorse and heather. Julie and I agreed to head over to look for Sabre.

We spent an hour or so calling for the dog, but eventually had to leave without making any contact. As we left, however, I had an idea. I fished an old coat of mine out of the back of the van and placed it on the grass in the quarry. My hunch was that if Sabre found the coat and recognised my scent, he might stay with it.

My plan worked. Early the next morning when the owner climbed the cliff path to the quarry, there was Sabre lying on the coat. The big dog wagged his tail and allowed a lead to be fixed to his collar. He was soon home for breakfast and from then on settled in well to life in his new home.

Sabre never again tried to run away and enjoyed a long and happy life. But the dog I was trying to capture now was a different case altogether. Rea seemed mentally disturbed, which made my job really difficult. As she moved unpredictably from place to place, it made it well-nigh impossible for me to set up a cage trap.

After a week of sightings from all around the area, we were no further ahead, although we had tried various methods of catching her. Rea seemed to identify my van from a distance, so I could never drive too close without her running off. I tried letting Julie or one of the girls walk towards Rea, talking to her and offering her food, but the dog would have none of it and kept her distance. Soon she was the best-known dog in the Perranporth area. She turned up on the beach, in gardens and on the roads. The one consolation was that, so far, at least, we had no reports of any aggression or damage. I was still concerned, though. I kept wondering what would happen if she found herself cornered on the beach or in the town, perhaps by a child. She was such an unpredictable dog she might easily attack.

Then one evening a neighbour phoned to tell us that a German shepherd had been seen entering the wood about half a mile from the centre. Julie and I immediately set off with our own dogs. We drew a blank, although a quantity of rabbit fur under a hedge suggested Rea may have been around and made a kill.

Over the next few days our dogs showed a lot of interest in the wood, sniffing around and scent marking. We suspected that Rea was still in the immediate area, but there was no response to our calls. More in hope than great expectation, I began leaving a bowl of meat out in the evenings. I thought this might tempt the dog to stay close by. The meat was always gone in the morning, but – as Karen, Sue and Julie kept saying – that could just as easily have been a badger or a fox taking advantage of a free meal.

And then for a while it went quiet. There were no reported sightings of Rea at all. This, to me at least, suggested she had made a semi-permanent home in the wood, so I decided to set up a large cage trap there.

Again, the results were frustrating. All we caught was a disgruntled fox, which rushed off when released, with his tail fluffed up like a bottle brush. I was still convinced that Rea was in the woods, however. Sure enough, the very next evening we caught sight of her standing on the edge of the wood, but as soon as I called her name the dog ran off into the shelter of the trees.

I was getting nowhere, so I decided to contact Rea's previous owner. 'Perhaps she'll respond to her,' I said to Julie.

'Worth a try,' she agreed.

The visit was arranged, and the elderly lady walked, with some difficulty, around the field bordering the wood calling Rea's name. Although we glimpsed Rea between the trees, she showed no signs of recognising her owner, so we eventually called it a day, gave the lady a cup of tea and drove her back to her home.

By now things were getting pretty desperate. Ten days had elapsed since Rea had run off and we still seemed no closer to catching her. To add to my worries, I developed a fairly severe attack of bronchitis and was confined to bed for a day or so.

I was still lying there when Rea appeared closer to home. Late one evening Julie was looking out of the bedroom window when she spotted what looked like the shape of a dog standing by the gate that led into the compound. It was lashing down with rain, blowing a gale and too dark to be certain it wasn't one of our own dogs. Even so, Julie felt instinctively that it was Rea trying to get back into the compound. She knew she had to act fast, so she put on her waterproofs and collected a blanket from Rea's kennel. Seeing there was no longer any sign of the dog at the gate, she set off to the wood, a quarter of a mile away, through the driving rain.

Starting at the place where we had several times spotted Rea entering the trees, Julie put the blanket on the ground and dragged it home to the farm, leaving a scent trail. Back at the farm, she pulled the blanket through the gate into the compound. She then placed a bowl of meat on the centre lawn and left the gate open, before returning to the house and changing out of her wet clothes.

I was blissfully unaware of what was happening, having dosed myself up with paracetamol and fallen into a deep sleep. At about 4 a.m. I was wakened by the cacophonous din of all the dogs barking – our own and those at the kennels. Stumbling to the window, I could see that the centre's lights were off. Yet in spite of the gale, which was roaring around the house, I thought I could hear Julie's voice shouting from the compound. I hastily flung on my trousers, pullover and a waterproof jacket, and left the house, wheezing and coughing.

Julie had heard the dogs howling and barking. Suspecting that Rea had gone into the compound, she had run across the garden into the centre, shutting the gate behind her. Her instincts proved correct. Sure enough, Rea had returned, but there was no way that she was going to allow Julie to catch her and had tried to escape from the compound, only to find that the gate was closed. She had then sat by the gate refusing to let Julie get past her. Julie had no keys with her, so could not let herself into any of the buildings to put lights on or phone me, so in desperation she had resorted to shouting in the hope that I would hear and come to her rescue.

I yelled to Julie and, once I understood what was happening, climbed over the compound fence. Julie was drenched and shivering, so I quickly unlocked the office, put on all the lights and found her towels and a blanket to wrap round herself while I dealt with Rea.

Next to the back gate was the bird-cleaning unit. I put the lights on in the unit and opened the end door nearest to the cringing dog. Then, walking around behind the dog, I called her name. As I expected, Rea ran from me straight into the bird unit, where she was trapped. Shutting the unit door, I left the dog to settle down and went back to the office to let Julie know she could go back to the farm.

Taking a grasper, I went back to the bird unit and

confronted Rea, expecting to experience problems. But she was a dog full of surprises. This time she wagged her tail and allowed me to clip a lead on her collar and take her to a kennel. In spite of being on the run for nearly two weeks, she seemed remarkably fit and was not unduly hungry.

All this took the best part of half an hour, and by the end of my exertions I felt completely spent. I had forgotten the bronchitis, but now I started shaking and realised that I was wet through, regardless of my waterproofs. Staggering back to the house, I found Julie drinking a cup of tea and joined her in the kitchen, sitting with my back to the warm Aga.

Fortunately, neither of us suffered any lasting problems following our hectic night. My bronchitis cleared up after a few days and did not develop into pneumonia, as it well might have done. Sadly, things did not work out so well for Rea. We kept a close watch on the dog's behaviour over the following weeks, but there was something very wrong. Sometimes she would be a happy, wagging dog, ready to be taken for a walk, always now on a lead of course. But there were also times when, instead of giving her normal welcome, she would cringe in her kennel, seemingly unable to communicate. Our vet suspected that Rea was suffering from a brain tumour and advised that she should be put to sleep. He said there was no way that we could send her out to a new home. We knew he was right. He just confirmed the suspicions I'd had all along. It was another example of an owner leaving us with a dog without giving us the full story, either deliberately or not. So for the sake of everyone involved, we agreed to call it a day.

Working with animals has its share of sad moments, times when unpleasant decisions have to be made. As an RSPCA centre, however, not only the animals we were putting up for adoption had to be considered, but also their owners. Happily, in the majority of cases things worked out well. Since we'd opened, hundreds of unwanted or abused cats and dogs had found caring new homes and settled down to enjoyable lives. In the case of poor old Rea, there was not to be such a happy ending.

CHAPTER FOUR

A Whiff of Trouble

Karen, Sue and I were on our knees scrubbing the floor of the bird-cleaning unit when a voice in the open doorway made all three of us jump.

'Morning, Mr Harper. Haven't caught you at a bad time, have we?'

We turned to see not only the uniformed figure of the director general of the RSPCA, but what looked like another half a dozen people entering the unit behind him. The inspection was obviously taking place earlier than expected.

'Er, no,' I said, clearly flustered as I got myself to my feet. 'Not unless you mind seeing us dressed like this.' The two girls and I had made an early start, slipping into our messiest overalls to do as much last-minute cleaning as possible in advance of the inspectors' arrival, which we'd been expecting mid-morning.

The bird-cleaning unit had been our biggest worry. The

rest of the pens and aviaries were in pretty good condition, but with a few birds still passing through the cleaning-up process, the unit needed a thorough washing down. We'd guessed that an hour's work cleaning the tiled floor and metallic surfaces would see the place looking presentable. Unfortunately, we hadn't bargained on the inspection team arriving this early.

They've come early to catch us on the hop, I thought to myself, glancing at the clock, which showed it was just 9.30 a.m. And they've succeeded too.

The director general did his best to put my mind at ease. 'Don't worry, Mr Harper, we know you've been up to your neck the past couple of weeks,' he said, turning to address the rest of the visitors, who had by now shuffled into the unit. 'The storm three weeks ago brought in – what was it? – two hundred birds, wasn't it, Mr Harper?'

I nodded from the sink, where I was trying to wash my hands as fast as I could manage. 'That's right. Guillemots and razorbills mostly, but quite a few gulls.'

The director general introduced the rest of his team, which consisted of a vet from the RSPCA and a few other officers specialising in different areas of the society, from funding to building and maintenance. It was clear they were all keen to get to work.

'You took in around two hundred birds last month, you say. How many did you manage to return safely to sea?' one of the committee members, a grey-haired man in a tweed suit, asked.

'Around seventy-five per cent,' I said. 'Which is pretty

good. As you can see, we are still dealing with the last of them.'

'Yes, I see,' he said, deep in thought for a moment. 'Seventy-five per cent. So twenty-five per cent perished, then,' he added, making a note on the clipboard he was carrying with him.

'Well, yes. That would be right,' I said, a bit alarmed by the tone of his questioning.

As Karen and Sue excused themselves and headed off to get washed and changed, I offered to give the visitors a quick run-through of the bird-cleaning process.

'That would be very helpful, Mr Harper,' the director general said, giving me a reassuring nod. 'It might help us understand what you're up against.'

I picked up a guillemot that had had its first wash but was still stained here and there with mottled, sooty patches of residual oil. 'As you can see, the oil permeates every inch of the bird's plumage,' I said, holding back its wing. 'It even gets into the joints here.'

'How many cleanings does it take to get them fit to return to the wild?' a lady in a raincoat asked.

'Well, normally two, but occasionally three. They can't take much more than that, so if that doesn't do the trick, the prospects aren't good, I'm afraid.'

This guillemot was ready for its second cleaning, so I went through the process in front of the watching audience.

'Looks like slow work,' another of the visitors said.

'It is. Luckily we've got some excellent volunteers who are willing to put in the hours,' I said.

As I finished off, Karen arrived with a tray loaded with teas. I chatted with my guests for a few moments about the bird-cleaning unit before the director general drained his cup and indicated it was time to get on with the tour of the centre. I decided to leave them to their own devices. It was important to let them make up their own minds. I made my excuses and headed towards the office.

I knew I had nothing to fear. We ran a good, professional operation and worked to the highest standards, always putting the welfare and safety of the animals first, but that didn't stop me worrying. It was probably something to do with my days in the RAF in the 1950s, when inspections really were something to dread. Our commanding officers would arrive in our billets expecting everything to be absolutely perfect – boots shining so you could see your reflection in them, every bit of kit polished and in working order. Such was the mortal fear the officers struck into us, very few failed to meet their high standards. I had fallen foul of the CO once, however, and it was an experience that was still etched in my memory.

At the time, I'd been a dog handler with the RAF police at their base in Trerew, near Newquay, patrolling the wireless station at night. My unsocial hours meant that I slept during the day. This didn't deter the CO, however, who would regularly conduct his inspections while we were sleeping.

On this one occasion he found three or four of us in our beds – lying to attention – everything shipshape and in its place, and the floors gleaming. Of course, none of us was really asleep and we watched him through half-opened eyes.

The CO walked around flicking his pace stick as he went. He was seemingly satisfied with what he saw and was about to leave when he noticed a small brass ring set into the floor. It was the handle of a trapdoor, beneath which was a compartment that had at one time been used to store ammunition. Something about this part of the floor had clearly caught his attention. Carefully placing the tip of his pace stick in the brass ring, the CO lifted the trapdoor and peered down into the space beneath. Later someone recalled seeing his face screw up in a look of pure disgust. The CO then reached down and produced a plate, upon which lay two rather pungent kippers.

One of the handlers had snatched a hurried breakfast before diving under the covers. Knowing the CO was on his way, he had placed the unfinished meal under the floorboards. Needless to say, the CO was not amused. All four of us were summoned to parade outside his office later in the day. We stood there shamefaced as he read the riot act. As punishment, we had our weekend leave withdrawn. I have never forgotten it.

No wonder I felt anxious about the RSPCA inspection, which continued all morning. Every section of the centre was gone over with a fine-tooth comb, and every member of our team was questioned about his or her particular areas of expertise. The visit would go a long way towards deciding what new equipment and facilities the centre would need in the coming year, so the inspectors were particularly keen to know how our existing premises were working.

My specialism was birds, so as I rejoined the touring party, one of the inspectors quizzed me about the aviaries. He seemed very knowledgeable. He was interested to know what types of aviaries suited the various species and their dietary needs. He was especially interested in a black swan we had in residence. One or two of these birds came to the centre each year, usually as strays. Black swans are from Australia and, as a species that is alien to this country, are supposed to be controlled so that they do not become feral. People who keep black swans on their private lakes are required, by law, to pinion any cygnets – remove the end joint from one wing – when they are a few days old to prevent them flying away. It is a painless operation, but unfortunately not everyone abides by the rules and so the cygnets grow up full winged and fly off when their parents chase them off their lake in the autumn. They are smaller than the native mute swans, but very aggressive and can cause mayhem with other waterfowl during the breeding season.

The inspection was my chance to make a case for new equipment and changes at the centre. This year I was keen to rearrange the pens and aviaries so as to accommodate more inmates. I showed the inspectors the rough plan I'd scribbled out for the new, expanded aviary. They seemed sympathetic with my argument. I was pleased to see the man in the tweed suit making another note on his clipboard. Something positive this time, I hoped.

In the kennels, we discussed the number of dogs now

flooding into the centre as a result of people choosing completely unsuitable breeds as pets. Border collies headed this list. I'd lost count of the number of collies that had been brought to us by people who'd seen them working sheep on television and imagined they'd like them as a household pet. Of course, collies need constant handling, lots of exercise and ideally need to follow their hard-wired instinct to herd. When they get none of these activities, they grow into stressed, bored dogs and start misbehaving, tearing up homes, rounding on children and – in extreme cases – even delivering people a nasty nip. In the latter case the dog would all too often be branded a dangerous animal and either taken to the vet for euthanasia or to a rescue centre for possible rehoming. These, plus some other working breeds, provided a number of headaches for centre staff.

After a while the questions dried up, so I left our cat specialist, Vicky, to show the party around the cattery. It was busy as usual. There was a discussion about building some new exercise pens, as the cats could benefit from extra outdoor space. From there, we went on a tour of the general animal accommodation. As ever, we had plenty of unusual residents to stimulate the conversation.

In the small-animal unit, a silver-fox rabbit called Lugless Douglas caught the eye of one of the inspectors. The rabbit had been brought to us after having both his ears cut off with a pair of scissors by a child. He had been removed from the home and taken into care at the centre, where he was making a remarkably good recovery.

Unsurprisingly, Douglas touched a nerve with the inspection team. No one who saw him could fail to be moved by what he had suffered. For a few minutes the little rabbit sparked a heated debate on the knotty subject of animal cruelty and, in particular, children's ability to look after pets. Opinion was divided. Some felt very strongly that children couldn't be expected to look after pets, while others argued it was simply a matter of education, something the RSPCA was well placed to provide via school visits.

The argument was still in full flow when Sue put her head round the door of the small-animal unit. 'Sorry to bother you, Rex, but there's a man in reception with a badly injured fox. I think that you should see it right away,' she said.

Excusing myself from the inspection team once more, I headed to the office to find a man sitting holding on his lap the limp body of a partly grown fox cub. He looked distraught and his trousers were soaked in the fox's blood.

'I hit the poor fellow with the car,' he said. 'He ran right across in front of me. There was nothing I could do to avoid him.'

It didn't look good. The fox was barely breathing and had severe injuries to its chest, legs and head. As I bent down to examine it more closely, it lifted its head briefly, sending more blood gushing from its mouth, before flopping lifelessly back down. It was the end, I felt sure. I placed my hand on the fox's flank and couldn't feel a heartbeat. 'Sorry, mate,' I said to the man, 'but I'm afraid there's nothing we can do for this chap.' He looked crestfallen but I reassured him. 'You really mustn't blame yourself for what happened. You did all you could. Thank you for taking the trouble of bringing him to us,' I said. 'Foxes don't have a lot of road sense, I'm afraid.'

The poor man was bordering on tears as I took the fox's body from him, covering my overalls in blood in the process.

I called Sue and suggested that she rustle up a cup of tea and a bowl of warm water with a sponge to remove the worst of the blood from the man's trousers. Having put the fox away, I rejoined the inspection team in time to see them finish their tour of the compound back at the bird-cleaning unit. 'Sorry about the mess,' I said, looking down at my overalls. 'Someone just brought in a fox that had been hit by a car.'

'No need to apologise, Mr Harper,' the director general said. 'In fact it's we who should be apologising for taking up so much of your time. It's clear you're very busy.'

'No peace for the wicked,' I said.

'Well, far better to find you running around than standing twiddling your thumbs. A few months ago we visited another centre, which shall remain nameless, and the warden greeted us in his Sunday-best suit. Didn't go down very well at all,' he added. 'Not appropriate for this kind of workplace and made it look as if the chap had far too much spare time on his hands.'

'Oh, I see,' I chuckled. 'No danger of that here.'

'No, that has been quite obvious, Mr Harper,' he said. 'And that's exactly as it should be. Well done, and thanks for showing us around. You'll get our formal report in a few weeks.'

'OK. Look forward to it,' I said, lying.

A few minutes later, the final goodbyes and handshakes exchanged, the inspection team's cars finally pulled away and headed back up the road towards Truro.

'Thank goodness that's over,' Karen said, slumping into a chair in the office.

'You can say that again,' I agreed.

'What did you make of the chap in the tweed suit? Seemed a bit stern,' said Sue.

'Did a bit,' I replied.

'Couldn't stop making notes on his clipboard. I didn't think we were that interesting,' added Karen.

We were soon joined by Julie, who had obviously seen the visitors leaving. 'How'd it go?' she asked.

'Fine, I think.'

'Hope they didn't spend too much time in the bird-cleaning unit,' she commented.

'What do you mean?' I said.

'Well, there's a terrible smell in there.'

'That'll just be the cleaning fluid,' Karen said.

'No, it's not that. It's as if something has died.'

'What?' Karen, Sue and I chorused as one.

'It hit me as I passed the door.'

Karen, Sue and I looked at each other, nonplussed.

'But we cleaned every flippin' corner of the place,' Sue said. 'It can't smell.'

I didn't doubt Julie had smelled something. I had lost my sense of smell many years earlier while working in a knitting mill in Truro. I'd been allergic to the woollen dust there which had caused polyps to grow in my sinuses. It had taken two operations to remove them, after which I'd been left unable to savour even the strongest countryside aromas. Julie's nostrils were far more sensitive than mine. So all four of us headed back to the unit.

Inside, Julie sniffed around like a well-trained gundog. Eventually her nose led her to below a high shelf. 'It's coming from here,' she said.

'What's up there?' said Karen.

I grabbed a stool and climbed up. At first I couldn't see anything, but then, tucked away right at the back of the shelf, I saw a white metal bowl. As I pulled it towards me, the stench hit even me. 'Oh, God,' I said. 'That stinks.'

The bowl was full of sprats, obviously intended for the birds at the height of the oil-spill crisis a couple of weeks back. Somehow it had been left on the shelf and forgotten. The sprats were now in an advanced state of decay and were covered in a white coating of mould.

'Oh, yuck, disgusting,' said Sue, backing away. 'How on earth didn't we spot that?'

'Did any of the inspectors come over this end of the unit?' Julie asked.

Karen, Sue and I looked at each other for a moment.

'Erm, no, I don't think so,' I said.

'Well, you might have got away with it,' Julie said.

'So who put it up there, anyway?' asked Karen.

'Well, I'm too short to reach,' said Sue.

'So am I,' added Karen.

I felt all their gazes falling on me. I genuinely couldn't remember placing the bowl there, but it wasn't beyond the realms of possibility that I had. I decided to do the honourable thing and fall on my sword. 'I think it might have been me,' I said sheepishly.

'Well, there's nothing we can do about it now,' Julie said.

'Do you think it'll count against us, Rex?' asked Sue, as we walked back to the office.

'Might mean loss of weekend leave,' I muttered to myself.

'Eh?'

'Oh, nothing. Hopefully not.'

CHAPTER FIVE

The Pied Piper of Perranporth

As I climbed down the stairs of the darkened cellar, the floor below me seemed alive with movement. Scanning it with my torch, I saw what seemed like hundreds of creatures darting in and out of the light.

'What have we got here – rats?' I asked Mike, the inspector with whom I'd travelled to the house this morning.

'Yup. And plenty more besides, I'd guess,' he said.

We'd been told to visit the house on the edge of St Ives by the chief inspector. After complaints from neighbours, it had been visited by a team from the RSPCA a week or so earlier. They had apparently discovered the property overrun with a variety of rodents – all living in utterly squalid conditions.

It wasn't an uncommon problem. Furry creatures like hamsters, gerbils, tame rats and mice are very popular as pets with families all over Cornwall. But as animals that breed indiscriminately and in large numbers, they can present a real headache for the careless owner. I had encountered many families who had suddenly found their homes overrun by pets.

To be fair, most of the problems stemmed not from the owners but the pet shops and their inability to distinguish properly the sex of these animals. I'd heard countless stories over the years of pairs of furry pets that had been sold as members of the same sex but had promptly started doing what came naturally and produced litters. Before they knew it, the unsuspecting owners had been overrun with animals and had headed back to the pet shop to complain. Unfortunately, their complaints would often fall on deaf ears. While there were reputable shops who took the unwanted additions in, they were sadly few and far between. Most sent their customers away with a shake of the head, leaving them with perhaps two dozen mice or half a dozen gerbils to dispose of. Again, many people would try to do things in the right way by placing an advert in the local paper or a notice in the local post office window. But when this failed – as it usually did – they would be faced with a harsh choice. The more responsible owners would turn to us for help and advice. The rest would take their unwanted pets out into the countryside and dump them, almost certainly condemning them to a quick and probably violent death.

As a result of this all-too-common problem, we tried our best whenever possible to take in these surplus furries. Even if they didn't find a new home, they would

– if the worst came to the worst – meet a humane end when we put them to sleep.

The house we'd been called in to clear out, however, was another story altogether. As Mike and I picked our way through the darkened cellar, the picture that was emerging was beyond anything we had dealt with in the day-to-day course of our business. The situation here was completely out of control. Clearly a large number of animals had been allowed to multiply at a prodigious rate. Picking our way around the large, musty-smelling cellar, we concluded there were well in excess of a hundred mice, rats and gerbils living there. The rats and gerbils were, in the main, contained within the dilapidated cages. It quickly became obvious, however, that a lot of the mice had managed to escape and were living, and breeding, in the cellar.

Our job was to collect the entire population of animals and remove them both for their own welfare and for health and safety reasons. Armed with torches and a variety of carrying boxes, Mike and I set about the task. We both knew it was going to be a long and tricky process. The ceiling was less than five feet high, forcing the pair of us to stoop awkwardly as we began gathering up the rodents.

As the smallest creatures in the property, the mice were predictably the most elusive. Both Mike and I were soon cursing like troopers as the little creatures slipped from our grasp on a regular basis. We were both wearing heavy gloves, which sometimes made getting a firm grip difficult. The smallest of the mice were able to capitalise on this by wriggling their way free, often without our even noticing. Even if we did spot them, they knew the cellar so well they headed straight for its darkest recesses, where they disappeared without any hope of us finding them again.

Adding to our troubles, the cellar had a greasy stone floor, which made it difficult to move around with any speed. So as we tried to catch the furry hordes roaming the place, we were both slipping and sliding around like a pair of silent-movie comedians. It must have made quite a sight. I was secretly glad there was no one there to record it, as, I'm sure, was Mike.

After a couple of hours we eventually managed to round up most of the mice, or so we thought. As we were clearing away the old cages and piles of rubbish that had accumulated against one of the cellar walls, we got a rude awakening. I moved away an old chest of drawers and what seemed like dozens of mice swarmed out, scuttling away once more towards the darkest parts of the cellar.

'I don't know about you, but I'm for calling in the Pied Piper,' I joked to Mike.

'Call in who you like, Rex,' he smiled. 'As long as I don't see this bloody cellar again in my lifetime I don't mind.'

After a further hour we had gathered enough furries to take back to the centre. But with many, many more still scuttling around our feet, we were resigned to having to return again the following day.

*

It wasn't the first time I'd found myself conducting a frustrating chase of small rodent-like creatures. Far from it. I'd had some memorable experiences dealing with – and often pursuing – a variety of them over the years. Back in the days before we had the farm, Julie and I had been fans of hamsters as pets. When we'd lived in a flat that precluded us from keeping larger animals, we'd had a female hamster called Ushie who'd become a memorable character and source of entertainment to us. Ushie had been a great hoarder and would constantly be on the lookout for any spare food, which she could stuff into her cheek pouches and carry off to her nest. She had the run of the flat and would show great determination in her foraging. She even developed a trick in which she would climb up the walls by pressing her back against furniture that was against the wall and using her feet to climb upwards like a caterpillar.

Ushie's adventurous spirit nearly cost her her life one Christmas. Rummaging around the house and its supply of festive goodies, she found a piece of chocolate and stuffed it into her cheek pouches, where it promptly melted. Julie discovered the poor thing choking and covered in chocolate. It took a lot of cleaning and syringing of her cheek pouches with warm water to put her right.

If Ushie was a challenge, so too was the chipmunk we took in years later at Ferndale. Chipmunks are delightful pets, especially when housed in a large cage with access to branches or, better still, in an outside aviary with a dry shed fitted with nest boxes. In this sort of environment their amazing speed and climbing abilities can be appreciated to the full. Unfortunately, not every home has this sort of equipment and we often had chipmunks brought to us by owners who simply couldn't give them the right home.

On one memorable occasion the RSPCA centre welcomed a chipmunk called Sonny. He was an extremely lively character and at one point escaped from his cage. He proved by far the most difficult animal I had ever had to recapture. Sonny could move like lightning – and seemingly in defiance of gravity. Whenever I got anywhere near him he would fly up the walls and across the ceiling, always just ahead of the large fisherman-style net I would brandish in pursuit of him.

I had spent the best part of half an hour chasing him around when I finally thought I'd cornered the hundred-mile-an-hour rodent. Just as I was closing in, however, one of our volunteer helpers 'helpfully' decided to come into the shed via the outside door. As quick as a wink Sonny had gone out into the garden.

'Oh, well done. That's the last we'll see of him,' I said to the shamefaced lad.

The wilds of Cornwall would be no place for a chipmunk to survive alone. Sonny would be easy meat for any predator. I marked it down to experience and made a note to myself to erect a new sign for all the doors warning, 'Please Knock Before Entering – Chipmunks May Escape.'

Life at the centre was always full of surprises, however, and one of the biggest occurred the very next morning when I was feeding some seabirds on their fibreglass pond at the edge of the compound.

The pond was raised slightly off the ground, leaving a space underneath. It was from there that I was suddenly aware of a familiar face poking out: Sonny. The fugitive chipmunk emerged whisking his tail and looking extremely pleased with himself. He still wasn't quite ready to return to domesticity, however. When I extended an arm and tried to grab him, he bolted. Even so, I guessed that he would be lured back to the centre quite easily now and placed some peanuts inside a cage that locked automatically when entered. It took a couple of days, but Sonny eventually succumbed to temptation. He remained under lock and key until he was rehoused a week or two later.

Mike and I returned to the cellar in St Ives the following day. Conditions were a little better after the clearance operation we'd done the previous day, but it was still the devil's work to catch the remaining two dozen or so mice. The smallest of the mice had secreted themselves in the tiniest nooks and crannies, but by the end of the morning Mike and I were confident that we'd gathered the last of them.

Mike's relief was tangible. 'Thank heavens that's done,' he said. 'I was starting to think I'd spend Christmas down there, and my back was beginning to kill me.'

'It's all right for you,' I said with a smile. 'I've got to sort them all out back at the centre now.'

'Sooner you than me,' he said.

All joking aside, I did have a Herculean task ahead of me. The owner of the house had been charged with causing suffering through neglect. So that the case against him could be made properly, the animals had to be fully itemised. This meant the entire population of the cellar would have to be kept in our care until the court case was heard, probably in a month or more.

The various cages that Mike and I had taken back had been placed in one of our small-animal rooms. I decided that it would have to be devoted entirely to the promiscuous furries for the coming month. Many of the females were either pregnant or had litters, so we had to find dozens of individual cages to accommodate them. The twenty rats we'd recovered, mostly young ones, needed larger cages, while ten gerbils were accommodated in two large glass fish tanks with plenty of sand to dig in.

The hardest part of the job was sexing the various rodents. This was a long, laborious and testing process. Gerbils, in particular, are famously difficult to sex, mainly because the adult male's testicles are retained internally, which makes it very hard to tell its genitalia from those of the female. I'd had many a phone call over the years asking me how to differentiate between a male and female of the species. I'd jokingly advised one or two callers to shake the animal to see if it made a sound. 'If it lets out a muted rattle, it's a male. If it doesn't, it's a female, probably!' I'd teased them. The truth is, there's almost no foolproof method to tell the difference.

As if to confirm this, over the coming days I discovered

that gerbils I'd thought were male were suddenly trying to mount each other. One of the males produced a litter! For the next month it became a pretty well full-time job caring for them. But eventually the case came to court. The owner of the house was given a hefty fine and the animals were officially signed over to the RSPCA, which meant I was then free to begin relocating his menagerie. Apart from a few of the older mice, we were lucky to find homes for almost all of the rodents. I can't say I wasn't glad to see the back of them.

CHAPTER SIX

Shell-shocked

The animals we welcomed to the welfare centre could be a little like London buses at times. We wouldn't see a particular species for a year or so, then all of a sudden we'd be dealing with three different types of them in a matter of weeks. So it proved with the furry family during the period while the occupants of the cellar in St Ives remained under our roof.

One morning soon after their arrival I took a phone call from a lady asking for advice regarding what she called a 'long, tube-like animal' that had taken up residence under the roots of a tree in her garden. I guessed immediately what it was. Sure enough, when I visited the large town house on the coast near Fowey, I found a ferret poking its bright-eyed face out from between the tree roots.

Where the ferret had come from was a mystery, but of far greater concern to me as I inspected this one was the fact that it was female and heavily pregnant. Towns aren't a natural habitat for ferrets, so it wasn't feasible to leave her roaming the streets around here. It was also likely that the ferret would produce a large litter, which would have added to her problems, and almost certainly have doomed the young ferrets to a short life. It didn't take me long to decide I would have to bring the ferret back to the RSPCA centre with me.

Capturing the little creature proved easier than I'd anticipated, perhaps because her size limited her movement. After tempting the ferret out from her tree-root retreat with a piece of raw meat, I managed to pick her up without her attempting to bite me. I then set off with her back to the RSPCA centre.

We'd had several ferrets living with us at Ferndale over the years. At one time we'd kept three of them on the farm to deal with the wild rabbits that had begun multiplying in the fields and woods. The ferrets enjoyed the company of the family dogs and one particular male, called Hob, used to join us on walks around the countryside, scampering happily alongside the rest of us until he found a drain or hole to explore. We would then have to wait until he re-emerged, having explored the depths to his satisfaction.

In more recent years ferrets had become something of a fashion accessory. At one time they were kept solely for the purpose of hunting rabbits. They were usually housed in small hutches and fed on bread and milk with the occasional bit of raw meat thrown in. Then some bright spark in America decided that a ferret could be an ideal pet. The mini-boom in ferret ownership soon spread over here to the UK and pet shops were being deluged with requests for ferrets. For a while it seemed everyone wanted a pet ferret. Books were written on how to keep them, and producers of animal food brought out a 'ferret chow'. Ferret shows and even ferret racing became popular.

While there is no doubt that ferrets are delightful animals if handled correctly, there are drawbacks to having them in your home, which people tended to forget. They are, it has to be remembered, relatives of the polecat, which is famous for its ability to emit a foul-smelling secretion if it feels cornered or threatened. Ferrets can do this too, as many unsuspecting owners have discovered to their horror.

On this occasion, having safely driven the ferret back to Ferndale, I entered the office to find the place full of inspectors, including Les, the Cornish RSPCA's chief inspector, who was chatting to Karen and Sue.

'What's this, the Christmas party nine months early?' I joked.

Les was never one to resist a little light ribbing, so my opening gambit was all he needed. 'Ah, Rex, the man who can't smell a sprat under his own nose,' he said, to general laughter around the office.

I thought we'd managed to keep that particular story under wraps from the inspectors. 'Thanks, girls,' I said through gritted teeth. 'Remind me not to share any more secrets with you.'

I could see that Les was holding a sheaf of paper with

the official RSPCA insignia on it. Before I got a chance to ask him what it was, he was advancing towards me and patting me on the back. 'Anyhow, Rex,' he said, 'it looks like you got away with leaving the smelly fish in the bird-cleaning unit. I've got the official report on the inspection visit here and they've given you a five-star review. Well done.'

To say I was relieved was the understatement of the year. Ever since the inspection I'd had a nagging doubt at the back of my mind that it could have gone better. I knew a smelly fish wasn't going to be enough to get us closed down, but it hadn't stopped me worrying about a public ticking-off. I had visions of being asked to explain our lack of cleanliness at the annual general meeting or some other public place, but it appeared I'd been worrying over nothing.

Instead, the inspectors had declared themselves extremely happy with the standards at the Perranporth centre. They'd even praised our levels of hygiene. I headed to the house to tell Julie the news, almost forgetting to pop the ferret into the general-animal shed on the way.

Later that morning, our postman, Len, and I were deep in conversation when we were interrupted by an estate car pulling up outside the front gate. It was quite a sight. Not only was it crammed full of children, it was also packed to the gunnels with suitcases, sleeping bags and beach paraphernalia. As if this hadn't made the car look overloaded enough, camping equipment was strapped down on the roofrack and a couple of bicycles had been lashed on to the back.

'What do you reckon, Rex – this lot off on holiday?' Len said sarcastically.

'Not all of them, Len. I bet they want someone to spend their Easter here,' I replied, heading over to the car, from which an entire family of six was being disgorged.

As I suspected, one of the younger children was carrying a cardboard box. To judge by the care he was taking, it contained something rather precious. I was soon being introduced to a rather aged-looking tortoise.

'This is Tommy,' said the father. 'We were wondering whether you could keep him safe for a fortnight while we're away.'

Julie and I still had a reputation locally for taking in animals at home. We were quite regularly asked to look after pets for people who were infirm or on holiday. Over the years we'd welcomed a menagerie of creatures, from cats and dogs to ponies and exotic birds. We'd even played host to an axolotl, a very strange-looking character that is the juvenile version of the Mexican salamander. We'd occasionally regret it, but somehow we'd never quite learned the knack of saying no. We never asked anything for doing it.

Compared with some of the guests we'd had, at least Tommy looked relatively trouble-free. We happily agreed to watch over him for the fortnight. After his family had driven off, we gave him the freedom of the garden at the rear of Ferndale.

*

Tortoises have always been firm favourites both with myself and the family. Of course, our attitude to animals has changed enormously over the years since I first took an interest in them, growing up in Bath during the Second World War. There's no question in my mind that tortoises were badly exploited in those distant days.

As a boy, I can remember Woolworths in Bath selling tortoises. The poor creatures were on display in a glass-fronted counter – dozens of them, crawling over each other – and offered for sale at extremely low prices. I doubt very much that many of them survived in their new homes. Later, when I worked in a pet shop at weekends and holidays, consignments of tortoises would arrive, packed layer upon layer in tall wicker baskets. The animals on the top were usually in reasonable condition, but further down there would be some that had died, probably through suffocation. Many of the reptiles were underweight, and most had ticks attached to their legs and necks, which I spent long hours removing.

Today, of course, the importation of tortoises is strictly controlled. Years ago, however, there were very few restrictions on their movement, and as a result we often had strays brought to us.

Before we moved to Ferndale and were living at a nearby cottage called the Rosery with our small children, we had several tortoises brought to us. They were quiet, undemanding creatures on the whole and would often wander into the cottage, especially during the late autumn, when the weather was turning cold and they were looking for somewhere to hibernate. The children were fascinated by them. Today, the health and safety inspectorate would have a fit to see children and tortoises crawling around on the floor together, but back then the risk of children contracting things like salmonella were considered slim indeed, mainly because no one had even heard of it.

In the years that had followed, a steady stream of the creatures had arrived at our front door – often in curious circumstances. One farmer had been ploughing a field when he'd noticed a large tortoise that was just about to be sliced with the plough. Another was brought in by a motorist who found it plodding along in the middle of a busy road without a care in the world.

My experiences looking after tortoises had taught me several eye-opening facts about these fascinating creatures. For instance, I had been horrified at their mating habits when I first witnessed them. I was alarmed at the way the males would seemingly attack the larger females, biting their hind legs and following them around. It was quite shocking. Suddenly they would rush at the female, drawing in their heads at the last moment before contact was made, colliding with a dull thud. One friend saw this strange behaviour and wondered if tortoises suffered from 'shell shock' after all the buffeting. Another wag observed that the noise the male and female made when their shells collided sounded like a bonk. 'Maybe that's the origin of the word "bonking",' he laughed.

The behaviour of female tortoises could be even more bizarre. When they are in breeding condition and about to lay eggs, for instance, they often eat grit. They probably do this to aid digestion, but it can lead to problems, as Julie discovered once when we had builders in the cottage laying a new floor. One morning she walked out of the house to discover one of our resident tortoises eating a freshly mixed batch of cement. Goodness knows what would have happened if she hadn't quickly grabbed it and taken it to the kitchen sink. It wasn't easy to open the tortoise's mouth, but once she had managed to do so, Julie wedged a pencil there to prevent the tortoise snapping it shut again. Then, using a hypodermic syringe filled with warm water, she carefully washed out all the cement that she could see. She also made certain that the tortoise ate as much fruit as possible that day in the hope of counteracting the setting effect that the cement might have had. Her improvised treatment obviously worked. The tortoise showed no signs of problems and soon afterwards laid eggs that weren't made of solid cement.

We'd learned too that tortoises are independent creatures. One small tortoise went missing from the farmhouse garden, and although the family searched high and low for the roving reptile, it could not be found. Two years later and Julie was walking in our lower fields. There, meandering along the hedgerow was the wanderer, none the worse for being out of doors through two pretty cold winters.

A few days after our latest tortoise guest had arrived, Julie stuck her head into my office. 'Rex, come quick,' she said, looking rather perturbed. 'I think Tommy has drowned.'

'What?'

As we ran round the back of the house into the garden, Julie breathlessly told me what had happened. 'I went to look for him and couldn't find him anywhere,' she said.

'It was only as a last resort that I thought I'd look in the pond. And that's where I found him. Oh, dear, what are we going to tell that nice family if Tommy is dead?'

When we got to the pond, I quickly saw that Tommy was indeed in it, lying lifelessly at the bottom. 'That doesn't look promising,' I muttered.

'I thought tortoises were good swimmers,' Julie said, shaking her head.

'They are. He must have fallen in and exhausted himself trying to climb out,' I said.

'So what do you think happened?'

'Well, basically, he sank.'

'What on earth am I going to tell those people?' she said. 'They thought the world of the old thing. How are they going to take it when I tell them we let him drown?'

I kneeled down and carefully retrieved Tommy from the bottom of the water. When Julie held the tortoise, his head was hanging limply from his shell.

'We'll have to bury him somewhere,' she said.

We were scouting the garden for a suitable spot when Julie happened to look at her watch. 'Oh, my gosh, look at the time,' she said, suddenly realising it was time to take the children to school.

At that very moment I heard the phone going in the office, which I knew was temporarily unmanned. 'I'd better see who that is,' I said.

'We'll bury poor old Tommy later,' Julie agreed, leaving him lying in a secluded corner of the garden.

The phone call was from the police asking for help in removing a stray horse from the nearby main road. It only took a couple of minutes to lead the horse into a convenient field, where it was soon reunited with its owner, who had been in a Land Rover looking for it.

By the time I got back Julie had just returned from the school run. She looked, if anything, more agitated than when she'd left.

'Rex, can you give me a hand burying this tortoise?' she said. 'I can't face it on my own.'

As we walked over to the pond, I tried my best to console her. 'It's not your fault,' I said. 'It could have happened at any time.'

'Yes, but it happened while Tommy was here in our care. Or *my* care, to be more precise.'

When we got to the pond, however, there was no sign of Tommy.

'Where did you leave him?' I asked.

'Here, in this corner. Where the heck is he?' Julie said.

'Hold on,' I said, gesturing at the spot across the garden where the other tortoises had gathered. 'Isn't that Tommy?'

'What?'

Sure enough, there he was, lying happily in the morning sunshine without a care in the world as if nothing had happened.

'Good grief. It's a miracle,' said Julie, beaming.

'A small one, yes.'

It was a couple of days before Tommy's owners returned from their break. When they came we didn't mention a word of his little accident, and it certainly didn't have any lasting impact on him. He came to stay with us on several other occasions, although he never strayed near that pond again.

CHAPTER SEVEN

Flying Visits

The lady was so distraught she had already worked her way through half a box of tissues. 'He is the love of my l . . . l . . . life,' she blubbered, dabbing away at her eyes. 'You will, take c . . . c . . . care of him, won't you, Mr Harper?'

'Of course we—'

'I don't know what I'd do if anything happened to my poor little P . . . P . . . Pierre.'

A rather grand elderly woman in a tweed suit, feathered hat and pearls, she had arrived at the front door of the house during my lunch break. I'd greeted her with a cup of tea in my hand but she'd been too emotional to notice that her timing might not have been perfect.

'I hear you take in pets while their owners have to go away,' she'd said, the tears already welling up in her eyes as she invited herself in. 'I have to go to London for three days and need someone to care for my darling Pierre.' She'd then proceeded to spend five minutes working herself up into a state, seemingly unwilling to stop fretting about her beloved Pierre, whoever and whatever he was. It was only now that she was, finally, beginning to calm herself.

'So you think you'll be able to cope with him, do you?' she said, the sobs subsiding slowly.

'I do.'

'Are you sure?'

'Yes.'

'All right, then, I shall go and get him from the car.'

I'd encountered people who were attached to their animals over the years and many who worried and pined about being separated from their pets when they stayed with us, but I had never seen someone work themselves into such a state about being apart from their pet for three days.

Julie and I had been so overwhelmed by the lady that we had simply sat there listening to her, unable to ask any questions. Unbelievably, we didn't even know what sort of animal she was talking about.

'What do you reckon it is? A dog, it has to be a dog,' I said, finally getting a chance to talk when the lady disappeared to her car.

'No, I think it will be a budgie,' Julie replied. 'Or a chimpanzee.'

'Now I know you're taking the mickey,' I said.

Our fits of laughter were interrupted by the sound of the lady returning through the back door.

'Oh, here she comes. We'll soon find out,' whispered Julie.

It was all we could manage not to burst out laughing when the lady reappeared in the kitchen. Pierre was a duck, or more precisely, a white drake.

'Here he is,' she said, stroking the bird endlessly. 'The love of my life.'

It was another five minutes before she'd managed to drag herself away, her lips quivering as she waved her umpteenth final farewell.

The lady was typical of a particular kind of animal lover, a breed of person whom – despite their best intentions – could be the bane of our lives. We are, it is often said, a nation of animal lovers. Yet over the years I had seen many examples of people who, like Pierre's owner, had taken that love to almost ridiculous extremes. This lady may have been the most histrionic of them, but she was far from the worst offender. At least she wasn't doing her animal any harm, as far as I could ascertain, anyway.

To my mind the biggest menace were those who saw themselves as modern-day versions of St Francis of Assisi. They would take it upon themselves to save every animal in the world and start accumulating creatures of all kinds, regardless of whether they had any experience caring for them. Invariably they did not and quickly found they couldn't cope with the work and cost involved.

The most common of these were people who set themselves up as cat or dog sanctuaries. They would take in every stray that came their way, which given the feral cat population in Cornwall, often meant they were soon surrounded by enough animals to fill Noah's Ark. The idea of neutering these animals would never occur to them, of course. So before they knew it these people were being overrun by litters of kittens or puppies as well. The end result was chaos.

On several occasions over the years we'd been called in to help people who had found themselves overrun by large numbers of cats or dogs. They were almost always kind, decent souls who had set out with every good intention. But the bottom line was that when things got to this point, their animals could be suffering badly from the effects of overcrowding, in-breeding and a general lack of veterinary care.

Horses, too, were animals that often became the subject of obsessive interest. We were once called in to a smallholding near Penzance that had more than fifty horses of differing ages and sizes wandering around its acreage. It turned out that the elderly lady who lived there had begun taking in unwanted ponies from rescue centres and uncaring homes a few years earlier. With money tight from the outset, she hadn't been able to castrate the colts and had soon found herself welcoming several foals each year. As was often the case in these instances, the lady lived alone and had given no thought to what might happen if she fell ill or died. When she'd been taken to hospital with a heart attack, the horses had been left to their own devices, with disastrous consequences. When we arrived, two or three of them were close to death. One had to be put down humanely.

Closer to home, I had a friend who also lived alone and died rather suddenly, leaving behind a collection of horses, ponies, a donkey, dogs and several birds. The property was left to a relative, who wanted all the livestock removed as soon as possible but had no intention of helping out with the disposal of the animals.

Another, far more caring, relative and I got together and spent an age trying to find homes for the animals. We got there in the end, but some of the horses were pretty aged, as was the donkey, so it was hard going. After that I'd taken an even dimmer view of misguided animal lovers.

After finally finishing my lunch, I took Pierre the drake out to the yard, where I intended placing him with the farm's other poultry. He was only with us for a few days. I didn't envisage him needing a great deal of extra care.

Despite the high emotions of the separation, the drake didn't seem unduly perturbed by the absence of his doting guardian. In fact, he seemed to revel in the freedom he now enjoyed. Released into the yard, he began by tucking into a healthy meal of corn that had been scattered on the ground. When he was finished, he flapped his wings and wandered off in the direction of the garden.

He was certainly a fine-looking bird, gleaming white with a yellow beak and legs. And he was extremely tame. Unfortunately, this meant that he had no idea of how to behave around other birds.

It wasn't long before he ended up in trouble. Exploring

the yard, Pierre strayed into an area where several hens were enjoying a dust bath under the hedge. One of the hens caught his eye and before she knew what was happening the big drake had grabbed her by the neck and jumped on her back in an attempt to mate.

The hen was not amused, and nor were the rest of her flock. Somehow shaking Pierre off her back, she ran off minus several feathers, pursued by the rest of the hens and a very frustrated drake.

Having met his owner, I wasn't surprised that the drake didn't know how to interact with other birds. I didn't know for sure, but I had a pretty strong idea that he had been humanised to a quite extraordinary degree by his doting 'mummy'. What I did know, however, was that he couldn't be allowed to harass and upset the rest of the farm like this, so I confined him to an enclosed pen for the rest of the day. He would have to entertain himself there. Pierre was still voicing his displeasure at his enforced separation from the hens as I headed back to the house.

There were times when birdlife seemed to dominate the day-to-day business at the centre. I only had to take a walk around the farm and the surrounding countryside to be reminded why.

The following morning was wild with a north-westerly gale blowing in from the sea, a typical Cornish start to a spring day. When walking some of the dogs in the fields, I couldn't help noticing that, as so often at this time of the year, the sky was absolutely full of birds: gulls, jackdaws and a small flock of our pigeons were all enjoying themselves by catching the thermals and soaring high up into the racing clouds. It was rather a stirring sight. They were flying, it seemed, for sheer joy, to experience the sensation of freedom and space that it gave them.

Birds have fascinated me since my childhood growing up in Bath, so I took a few moments to enjoy the aerial show. I was still taking it in when, suddenly, like a lightning flash, a tiercel peregrine dive-bombed the flock of pigeons at tremendous speed. Peregrines are extremely powerful and effective predators. Such was the accuracy and force of this one's dive, it hit one young pigeon so hard it completely decapitated it. If that was impressive, so too was the way it then held on to its prey with one foot and dropped out of the sky to land in a small field in the shelter of the disused railway embankment that runs at the bottom of our fields.

If the peregrine had imagined its morning's work was over, however, it was soon rudely awakened. Just as it began to pluck at the pigeon, over the embankment came a noisy quartet, made up of two ravens that were being hotly pursued by a pair of carrion crows. The latter were vocally accusing the ravens of crossing their territory, but the ravens – being ravens – were not taking the slightest notice of their smaller relations' complaints and were heading back to their nest on the distant coastal cliffs.

They were soaring effortlessly away when one of the ravens spotted the peregrine busily readying its breakfast in the field below. As one, they checked in their flight and dropped down. For a moment it seemed as if they would actually land on top of the peregrine, who at the last moment jumped to one side of the pigeon and stood hurling abuse at the ravens. Once more, however, the protests fell on stony ground. The ravens ignored the insults and started to examine the corpse. They would, I'm sure, have begun tucking in, had it not been for the intervention of another interested party.

Lexi, a German shepherd in our care at the centre, had been alerted by the noise and general commotion and had arrived on the scene. One of the ravens had picked up the pigeon and was readying itself to fly away when Lexi barked at it. The raven soon dropped its stolen breakfast and fled, but only after delivering a rather angry croak at the dog, who was now sniffing the pigeon with interest.

With the ravens gone, the peregrine reappeared. It was working out its frustration in a frenzied display of flying, one moment screaming as it skimmed feet from the ground and the next spiralling up into the clouds only to dive down again. Watching the peregrine, I guessed it was biding its time, ready to dive and perhaps steal the pigeon from under the nose of the dog if Lexi moved away for a moment. Before it could strike, however, yet another predator, who had been watching the whole sequence of events, intervened. I quite fancied roast pigeon for supper, so I quickly stuffed it into the pocket of my coat and headed back to the house.

I was passing the barn when I heard the sound of a speeding vehicle. A moment or two later I saw a Land

Rover pulling to a sudden halt outside the office and a man emerging carefully cradling a small box against his chest. He seemed concerned by whatever it was he was carrying, so I went to meet him.

'Can I help?' I said.

'Hope so. I found this while I was fishing,' he replied, lifting the lid off the box. 'I think it's a kingfisher. Doesn't look good.'

He was right on both counts. It was indeed a kingfisher, a young adult, and it certainly didn't look good. In fact, my first impression was that the floppy, sodden bird was dead.

'Let me have a look,' I said, taking the box from him.

Ever since I was a boy I'd been dazzled by the brilliance of kingfishers. Seeing one at close quarters was like looking at a living jewel, so intense and sharply defined are their colours. This one was no exception, with its brilliant blue and chestnut feathers. Its eyes, which should have been bright and inquisitive, seemed dull and lifeless, however. Only its dagger-like beak was making any movement. At least it was a sign that it was breathing, albeit ever so lightly.

'It's alive,' I said. 'But only just. Come with me.'

I headed straight for the treatment room, where I kept the most seriously injured of our birds. I wouldn't ordinarily invite a member of the public to join me, but in this case I was keen to know more about the circumstances in which the angler had found the bird. It might tell me more.

'I was fishing the Fal when I saw this flash of blue in

the leaves of a willow tree upstream of where I'd cast my line,' he explained. 'I dismissed it at first, but then my curiosity got the better of me and I walked along the riverbank to investigate. I couldn't believe it when I saw this little kingfisher dangling from a branch of the willow. When I looked closer, I saw it was suspended by a thin nylon fishing line, which must have got tangled round the branch.'

'No idea how the line got there, I suppose?' I asked.

'Well, it wasn't me. I was fishing further downstream and I didn't see anyone else on the bank. So, no. Must have been a freak accident of some kind.'

The angler said he had no idea how long the bird had been hanging there. Judging by the weakness of its fluttering, it must have been quite a while. It was obvious that the kingfisher was now exhausted and had all but given up on ever getting free.

'It was an effort to get him,' the angler told me. 'I waded into the river with a long branch that I found on the bank. I used it to lower the branch that was holding the kingfisher low enough for me to cut the line and grab it. I had a quick look but there was no obvious sign of a hook in its throat. The bird looked like it was dying,' he said. 'That's when I thought I'd better dash over here.'

The bird was so weak a thorough examination would have to wait, I decided. Instead, I placed the kingfisher on a towel inside a heated cage.

As I walked with the angler back to his Land Rover, I thanked him for his initiative in bringing the bird in. A greater contrast to the elderly visitor I'd had a couple of days back I couldn't have imagined. Pierre's owner would never have displayed such a combination of common sense and selflessness, I felt sure.

'You've given it a chance of living it wouldn't have had otherwise,' I reassured him as he left. Deep down, however, I knew that chance was still pretty slim.

When I returned to the kingfisher a few minutes later – after a quick dash to the kitchen to give Julie the pigeon I'd acquired for our supper – I fully expected it to be dead. To my surprise and delight, I found the patient was not only alive but sitting up and looking around at the room.

'Well, well,' I said. 'You've perked up a bit, haven't you.'

Checking the bird, I was pleased to find that its body weight was normal and its plumage in immaculate condition, a sure sign that its overall health was fine. My concern now was removing the hook that had got the bird into trouble in the first place. Hard as I looked, I could see no obvious sign of it. Where had it lodged?

The fishing line was extremely fine, which made me suspect the hook might be very small, possibly the type of simple one used by young boys fishing for minnows. I had used them many times myself when I was a lad. This made me wonder whether this might be the explanation for the freak accident. Perhaps the minnow had escaped with the hook and the length of line attached to it, only to fall prey to the hungry kingfisher. There was no way of telling for sure, of course. What mattered now was removing the hook.

Very carefully I moved my finger down the feathers of

the bird's neck, feeling for any slight bulge. Sure enough, about halfway down I could feel the bent metallic form of a tiny hook through the skin. This was a far from uncommon occurrence. I'd removed hooks from the throats of many a bird over the years. I knew it should be possible to retrieve this one.

The first thing was to locate the back of the hook, then angle it round so that the point could be pushed through the skin. I did this, then slid the hook out and pulled the nylon line out too. In no time at all the kingfisher was back in its hospital cage seeming pretty well unfazed by its experience.

Adult kingfishers are not easy birds to keep in captivity, mainly because they normally only eat live, moving prey and are therefore very difficult to feed, so I didn't want this one to remain at the centre any longer than was absolutely necessary. This was going to be a flying visit and nothing more.

That night as I did my rounds, I was amazed at the recovery it had made. The bird's condition was so good and its health had improved so dramatically I decided to release it the following morning. I went to bed rather looking forward to it.

I'd barely taken the first sip of my morning tea when there was a loud rapping on the glass of the back door. I could tell from the silhouette in the frosted glass who it was. The feathered hat was a giveaway.

'Good morning,' the tweed-suited old lady said, when I opened the door. 'I've just got back from London and I couldn't wait any longer to see my darling Pierre. How has he been?'

The short answer to that question was simple. 'He's been confined to barracks. For sexually harassing the hens,' I was tempted to say, but I didn't see the need to tell her this and instead reassured her that he was fine. 'I think he's enjoyed his little holiday,' I said.

'Oh, good. I couldn't stop thinking about him all the time I was away.'

I knew from my previous encounter with the lady that she wasn't going to let me finish my morning tea in peace, so I ushered her out of the door into the yard to reunite her with her precious companion.

The previous day I'd given Pierre a second opportunity to interact with his fellow yard-dwellers but he'd quickly blown it. Once more, he'd made a beeline for the hens, scattering them to the four winds as they searched for a safe haven from the sex-starved drake. I'd done my best to integrate him, but I'd been forced to return him to solitary confinement. He was standing up in the isolation pen when I took his owner in to him.

'Oh, Pierre darling, you're on your own,' she said. 'Did you not make any friends?'

I was diplomatic. 'Pierre was obviously missing you, madam,' I said. 'He couldn't settle sleeping in the same pen as anyone else.'

'Oh, Pierre,' she said, close to tears now. 'I didn't sleep a wink either, worrying about you. Never mind. Mummy's here now. Let's get you home.' Scooping up the bird, she headed off to her car.

She was still clutching Pierre when she climbed into the driver's seat. To my astonishment, she then placed him on her lap, slipped the car into gear and drove off.

By now, Julie had joined me, having finished with her early morning rounds in the fields. 'What on earth's she doing?' she said.

'I've no idea,' I said. 'Have you ever seen anything like it?'

'I suppose that's what you call "ducking and driving",' she said.

We didn't stop laughing for the rest of the day.

With Pierre safely seen off the premises, I left for the banks of the Fal, heading for the spot where the fisherman had rescued the kingfisher the day before. At the far end of a small valley, I found what looked like the place he had described.

It was a beautiful morning, and an absolutely idyllic scene. The sun was breaking through the trees, dappling and dancing on the surface of the smooth rushing waters. Looking out across the river, I saw a heronry in the Scots pines. A group of half a dozen or so adult herons were gathered there, some carrying nesting material, others standing like grey sentinels by their nests. Around the fringes of the heronry, there were several little egrets, their plumage gleaming snow white in the morning sun. A few were taking advantage of the low tide to patrol the muddy edge of the river, wading into the water and every so often darting forward to snatch up small fish.

Herons and kingfishers pose no threat to each other; indeed they tend to live in harmony together, thriving in environments like this. I took the kingfisher out of the box and held it for a moment in my hand. The second I opened my hand the bird was away, flying straight as an arrow across the rippling surface of the Fal, to eventually perch in some low trees on the far bank, not far from the heronry.

I couldn't help but sit there for a few minutes, simply breathing in the scene. The little kingfisher immediately settled back into its home. Within moments it was darting from branch to branch, scanning the waters for prey. It would soon be back to its normal routine, I felt sure. Hauling myself up off the bank, I headed back to the centre, ready to resume my own routine. Not that anyone could ever call it normal, of course.

CHAPTER EIGHT

Whiskers Galore

After running some errands in Truro first thing, I arrived back at the centre to find the office empty, apart from one inspector, who was busy on the phone. I left him to it and headed out into the compound, making straight for the building that had begun to monopolise everyone's time these past few weeks.

The catteries were full to the brim at the moment with twenty or so stray, unwanted and ill-treated cats in residence. During the past couple of weeks we'd also taken delivery of five heavily pregnant strays, each of whom was in a pretty bad way physically. This quintet needed lots of attention because, if their size was anything to go by, they would each be giving birth to large litters. The five expectant cats were housed in the isolation unit, where they were being well fed and kept warm around the clock. Their litters would be arriving any day now.

As it turned out, however, it wasn't the pregnant strays that were preoccupying Karen, Sue and Vicky when I found them in the largest cattery. Instead, they were standing over another, rather pitiful-looking new arrival.

To judge by its coat, the large, blue Persian had just spent a year on a jungle safari. To say it looked like it had been dragged through a hedge backwards was the understatement of the year. Its long, thick hair was horribly matted, with sections sticking out stiffly, as if they had been spiked up with Brylcreem. It reminded me a little of some rather garish punk rockers I'd seen on television once.

'Oh, dear,' I said. 'That's going to take some combing out.'

'You can say that again,' nodded Vicky, who was standing over the cat looking perplexed. 'I'm not even sure where to start. I know he'll go for me the minute I put a comb anywhere near him.'

It turned out that the cat, known rather grandly as Prince Igor, had been brought in earlier that day by a lady from nearby St Agnes. The story she had recounted was all too familiar. What had entered her home as an adorable ball of playful fluff had turned into an unmanageable and temperamental nightmare. The problems had begun the moment the kitten had grown into a cat and started wandering outside, dragging its long-haired coat through the mud and overgrowth of the Cornish countryside. Its long coat had quickly picked up all sorts of debris and the cat soon needed almost daily grooming to stop its fur from matting. As anyone who has kept a long-haired cat will know, this can be long, laborious work and requires the cat's compliance. Prince Igor had always been a less than willing customer when it came to grooming and his owner quickly fell behind. It wasn't long before frustration set in on both sides. The more the lady tried to get the comb through the tangled coat, the more she began to hurt Prince Igor's sensitive skin. Things began heading in a downward spiral. By the end the cat was so scared of being groomed it would attack its owner or indeed anyone who tried to unlock its tangles. Hence Vicky's justifiable caution today.

With so many other feline customers in need of attention, we couldn't spend all day staring at the cat, so Vicky took a deep breath and moved in with a pair of scissors and a comb. The reaction was predictable. The moment she touched Prince Igor he began hissing savagely and lashing out with his claws, catching Vicky on the forearm with one of his slashing movements.

'Ouch! That hurt,' she said, growling at the miscreant. 'You're definitely not a real prince.'

Vicky wasn't one to be beaten easily. Quite the opposite in fact – she was a determined character who didn't like to come off second best to anyone. I could see she was readying herself for another attempt when I intervened. 'Let's leave him for today. Let him calm down tonight and I'll deal with him tomorrow morning.'

'What makes you think he'll be any better tomorrow?' Vicky protested.

'He won't be,' I said.

'So what's going to be different?'

'What will be different is that I will be using plan B.'

'Plan B?'

'Just wait until the morning. You'll see.'

Leaving Vicky to place the irascible Persian in a cage for the evening, I headed towards the part of the cattery where our pregnant strays were all billeted. They'd arrived from various points across the county in the space of a few days. One had been recovered from a rubbish dump, another from the roadside. All had been unceremoniously dumped by their heartless owners.

It never ceased to amaze me how uncaring people could be in abandoning pets that were about to produce litters, especially in the open countryside, as was often the case with the animals we were asked to help. Cats, in particular, are extremely vulnerable. Unless they are used to hunting for rodents and small birds, which many domesticated cats are not, they cannot hope to support themselves in these challenging surroundings. The fact that they are hampered with the extra weight of their unborn kittens makes life even more difficult for them.

Four of the five we'd been handed were young, almost kittens themselves, and had arrived at the centre in very poor shape. Two were starving and emaciated and – when they arrived, at least – incapable of caring for themselves, let alone a litter of hungry kittens.

The quintet had been with us for about a week now, and I knew their litters would be arriving imminently. Experience told me that there was every chance that once one gave birth, the other four would follow. So, as I checked them today, I was immediately drawn to the fact that one of them, a dark tortoiseshell, was lying in her cage purring away and occasionally turning round to lick herself. This was a sure sign that her contractions were under way. Things were on the move.

Unlike some other animals, cats rarely need supervision during labour. Felines are wonderful mothers and have an amazingly relaxed approach to giving birth. Given the freedom to roam, a prospective mother will often pace around for a day or so before her kittens are born, searching for what she considers to be the best place to make a nest. Our own household cats had quietly and efficiently given birth to healthy litters in airing cupboards and wardrobes.

Unfortunately, this wasn't an option available to these strays, but we had made sure their cages had sufficient space for the mother to move around a little and for her to accommodate the newborn kittens when they arrived. I made sure this cat's cage had a decent supply of water and was warm enough, then left nature to work its magic. I would check again in the early evening, by which time I fully expected to discover a litter of kittens suckling up to their mother.

The new arrivals would not be the only kittens at the centre. Before heading back home for a cup of tea, I decided to check on another of our recent arrivals, a rather troublesome male kitten that had been brought in two weeks earlier, around the same time as the pregnant cats. I'd received a letter about the kitten just that morning and so grabbed it from the office before heading off to his cage, which was in another of the catteries.

According to the owners, who had dropped the kitten off at the centre, they had been given him by some friends who lived in Scotland. He had travelled down from north of the border by train. When he arrived, he had been pleasant enough, but his behaviour had quickly become extremely strange. The kitten had resented being picked up and petted in any way and had scratched the family's young children quite badly when they tried to handle him.

He had been equally fractious when he arrived with us, and had also been behaving in a way that I found slightly odd. While safe in the confines of a cage in the cattery, the tabby and white kitten appeared quite ordinary and composed. So long, that was, as the cage door was closed. When the door was opened, however, the cat's whole demeanour changed. He would lie crouching in his bed with his ears flattened tightly against his head and his yellow eyes blazing, growling menacingly at the would-be intruder. Woe betide anyone who went near him.

Since his arrival, all the centre staff had tried in vain to make friends with the reluctant kitten, but each of us had ended up getting scratched, as the little animal lashed out with his claws. Vicky, always the best at coming up with witty names for our inmates, had quickly christened the kitten Claude. 'As in "The little bugger just clawed me again",' she said wryly.

Claude hadn't won any friends at the centre since arriving, but the little cat still intrigued me. There was something about him that I couldn't quite put my finger on and I'd asked Sue to find out more about the cat's background from the owners, who were perfectly intelligent and responsible and whom we knew quite well. As promised, they'd written, but, with so much going on, I hadn't yet had a chance to digest their letter. As I pored over it now, I began to see the kitten in a slightly different light.

'Have you read this letter about Claude?' I asked Vicky, who was seeing to another cat at the other end of the cattery.

'No. What does it say?'

'Well, it's quite interesting. It says that Claude was born on a farm in a pretty remote part of Scotland, near Inverness.'

'So?'

'Well, there are wildcats around there and I was talking to someone the other day who mentioned that they have been known to interbreed with domestic cats.'

'What, so you think he's a wildcat?'

'No. Half wildcat. I wouldn't be surprised if his father is wild and he's inherited his temperament.'

'But how come he's so placid in his cage? And he doesn't look like a wildcat. They've got longer legs.'

'You can't tell the difference when they're young. They look no different to domestic kittens. It's only as they grow up that their wild characteristics really begin to show through.'

'Hmm. It would explain a lot.' Vicky nodded. 'If he's part wild, it's little wonder he reacts the way he does when a human gets near him.' She paused before asking, 'So what are we going to do with him?'

'Not a lot, I suspect. We'll watch him for a while, but I think we should have him neutered as soon as possible, then let him go.'

'Go where?'

'We will try to get him a farm home, where he can live out of doors controlling the rodent population. Certainly he will never make a domestic pet.'

We were still discussing Claude's potential parentage when Karen arrived in the cattery with a concerned look on her face. 'You'd better come quickly,' she said. 'I think the cat's having problems delivering these kittens.'

The tortoiseshell cat I'd left to her own devices earlier on was now in a distressed state. She seemed to be in pain and couldn't settle down. One moment she would be lying in her bed licking herself frantically, the next she would be pacing around her cage and mewing plaintively.

I didn't like the look of this. She should have given birth by now. 'Give Julie a shout,' I said to Karen.

Within minutes Julie had appeared. She took one look at the cat and made her mind up immediately. 'Something's not right here,' she said. 'Give me five minutes to set up a cage in the kitchen, then bring her up to the house.'

Soon the expectant mother was in a cage by the Aga under Julie's watchful eye.

'We'll give it a bit more time,' she said, 'but if things get any worse, we'll have to call the vet.'

I had a lot of errands to run so left her to it. When I

returned to the house an hour later, I found the cat lying alongside a rather large kitten. 'Oh, she's got it out. That's great,' I said, relieved.

'It was a bit of a struggle,' Julie replied. 'It was the wrong way round. It was lying across the birth canal and was never going to get out.'

'No wonder she was in such pain,' I replied. 'So how did you do it?'

Julie proudly held up the obstetric instrument that had saved the day – her hand. 'I knew they were all going to die if it carried on, so I stuck my finger in the mum's birth canal and managed to turn the kitten so its head was facing the right way.'

'That can't have been easy.'

'No, it wasn't. I didn't think it was ever going to work. But the kitten helped out in the end. I think it wanted to get out of there. Once its head was in position, it slipped out easily.'

'It's a big 'un all right,' I said. 'How many more are in there, do you think?'

'A fair few,' said Julie. 'But I think the worst is over.'

By the end of the night we'd welcomed four more kittens into the world. We let mother and litter sleep soundly by the Aga overnight. I'd return them to the cattery the following morning.

Straight after breakfast I moved the new family and headed for another cage in the cattery, determined to tackle Prince Igor. I knew the best way forward was to mildly sedate the cat. So having let Prince Igor calm down a little, I ground a couple of sedative tablets and slipped them into a bowl of food. He was soon wolfing it down.

A few minutes later the hot-tempered Persian was lying on a table, too drowsy to offer even a token resistance. Grooming him was still a daunting task, I soon realised. It was going to be impossible to comb out the matts, which had become solid lumps of tangled fur, so I started working away at his coat with a pair of electric clippers, cutting away the clumps as carefully as possible. Even then it was very heavy going. His coat was so thick and matted the clippers regularly got stuck or so clogged up that they needed cleaning. Eventually, however, I was able to remove the cat's tangled coat right down to the skin.

The transformation was, it has to be said, remarkable. Half an hour earlier Prince Igor had been a mass of bedraggled blue hair. Now he was a semi-nude cat with just the hair on his head, legs and tail remaining.

As he began to emerge from his torpor and realise what had happened, the cat didn't seem to appreciate his new look. For the next few minutes he sat in his cage frowning at everyone. (Persians cannot help frowning. Their faces are made that way.) Fortunately, however, he hadn't lost his appetite and made short work of his dinner when it arrived.

When Vicky appeared in the shed to see how I'd got on, she was shocked at what she saw. 'Oh, my goodness,' she said, slack-jawed at the transformation. For a moment or two she simply stood there, wondering at the manicured creature. 'You know what we should call him?' she said, after a while, a mischievous smile forming on her face.

'Go on, then – what?'

'Shawn.'

CHAPTER NINE

Children and Animals

PLEASE
KEEP
YOUR
FINGERS
OUT

Midway through the morning the playgrounds and corridors of Redruth Secondary School were eerily quiet. Making my way through the entrance to the school secretary's office, I could see the classrooms full of pupils hard at work at their desks.

'Morning. I'm here to see Mr Jameson,' I said, announcing myself at the reception desk.

'Ah, yes. You're from the RSPCA centre, aren't you?' the secretary said, smiling. 'Come to collect our newest arrival. Let me show you the way to the science block.'

We'd had a call from the school at the start of the day. While waiting for the school bus that morning, a group of children had apparently discovered a tiny bird of prey shivering and looking distressed on the floor of the bus shelter. They hadn't known what kind of bird it was, but one of the children had had the foresight to put the bird in a small plastic box and had taken it to their science teacher, Mr Jameson, a keen birdwatcher. He'd identified it as a week-old buzzard and recommended someone call us.

I found the teacher in one of the science laboratories where a biology class was under way. A couple of boys were dissecting a dead mouse in one corner, while in another a girl had a dead locust pinned to a piece of board.

'Thanks for coming over so quickly,' Mr Jameson said. 'Let's get this bird out for you.' The class were still wrapped up in their various experiments and assignments. 'All right, children,' Mr Jameson announced, after a loud clap of his hands. 'Take a break from what you're doing while Mr Harper here has a look at our baby buzzard.' He then gestured towards a young lad at the front of the class. 'Come on, Ronnie, you discovered it. You can show Mr Harper.'

The boy walked over to a corner cupboard from which he produced a box lined with tissue paper and containing a tiny fluff-covered chick. I could understand why the children had been unsure of what it was at first. Young bird-of-prey chicks do look very alike. To the untrained eye, there were few signs that it was a buzzard rather than, say, a kestrel or a sparrow hawk. As a bird expert, however, Mr Jameson had correctly worked out its identity from the bird's size and age, which he'd accurately gauged at around a week.

Ronnie explained how he had found the bird and then his teacher invited him and the rest of the class to ask questions. They were soon flying at me from all directions.

'So why was it in the bus shelter?' asked one little girl.

'No idea,' I said, to disappointed looks. 'But my guess is that a predator, perhaps a crow, snatched it from its nest while its parents' backs were turned, then dropped it when it was in flight.'

'So it was its lucky day,' the little girl said.

'Certainly was. And it was lucky again that it landed near young Ronnie here.'

'So what will you do with it now?' asked another boy.

'I'll take it back to the RSPCA centre and we'll look after it for a few weeks.'

'What does it eat?' asked another child.

'Small pieces of raw meat,' I said. 'We keep some dead chicks frozen in our deep-freeze specifically for birds of prey.'

'Oh, yuck,' said one little girl, putting her hand over her mouth.

'But it will also eat insects and worms.'

'How long will it be with you, Mr Harper?' asked Ronnie, the bird's rescuer.

'Six to eight weeks, Ronnie.'

'And then what?'

'When we've built up its strength enough, we'll release it into the wild to fend for itself.'

After a few more minutes of this Mr Jameson brought the children's questions to a halt. 'Perhaps Mr Harper would agree to coming back to school one day to give a talk?' he said.

'It would be my pleasure,' I said, sensing an opportunity for a little free advertising. 'And if any of you are interested in coming to see how the buzzard here is getting on, we're having our annual open day this Saturday.'

A few moments later I was preparing to leave with the buzzard chick, which I'd transferred to a more secure carrying box.

'Oh, Mr Harper, by the way, we've given him a name,' Ronnie said.

'Oh, right. What is it?'

'Fury,' he said.

'Right, then. Fury it is.'

Saturday morning brought glorious weather: hot but with a soft, sweet-scented breeze. Perfect for our annual open day, or so I'd thought. As I emerged from one of the aviaries, where I'd been busy putting information notices on the cages, I heard Julie and some ladies from the RSPCA committee in animated conversation. In the days running up to the event, we'd been praying for fine weather. Now, it seemed the summery conditions were a problem.

'I'm worried, Mrs Harper,' said one lady, laying out the cake and refreshment table outside the office.

'Why?' Julie replied, looking puzzled.

'I don't think we have enough lemonade. If it's going to be as hot later on as everyone is saying, we're going to need a lot of lemonade.'

'Oh, don't worry about that,' Julie replied. 'I'll get

working on another batch when I've finished doing the table.'

The open day was always held around this time, at the end of May or the beginning of June. It was, in many respects, the highlight of our year: our chance to relax a little and meet the local community. It was also our neighbours' opportunity to see what went on behind the fence surrounding our compound.

As usual, everyone had arrived bright and early, eager to get on with the last-minute preparations. While Karen, Sue, Julie and I were busy making sure everything was in order in the catteries, aviaries, bird-cleaning unit and animal hospital, the RSPCA inspectors were laying out piles of literature for people to pick up and take home. The ladies from the committee, along with a few of the male members' wives, were putting the finishing touches to stalls selling plants, homemade cakes and pasties, and second-hand books. The lemonade crisis aside, everything seemed on course for the arrival of our first guests at around 10 a.m.

We'd been staging the open day for a couple of years now. We publicised it with flyers and by promoting it on the local radio station, BBC Radio Cornwall. Visitors would have an opportunity to talk to myself and the other centre staff, members of the Cornish RSPCA committee and some of the inspectors. Karen, Sue and I also offered people a guided tour of the centre, which was always popular, especially with the younger visitors.

Shortly after ten the first arrivals drove into the overspill car park we'd set up in one of our fields. It was a large family with four children and Sue and I were soon taking charge of the youngsters for a tour of the compound. The notices I'd put up on all the aviaries that morning gave full details of each cage's inmates. In the case of our ageing, vocal and rather eccentric raven, Odin, the notice was accompanied by a special request asking people not to poke their fingers through the wire of his cage.

Odin had lived with us for many years, becoming, to all intents and purposes, a member of the family. He had learned to talk and was an incredibly mischievous bird and loved nothing more than giving strangers a nip, preferably on the backside, but if that wasn't available, anywhere else.

This morning, with typical cunning, he had stuck his head close to the mesh and was encouraging people to tickle him with cries of 'Come on, then.' The response was predictable. Two of the young children in the group were already moving in close to the bird.

'I wouldn't do that if I were you,' I said.

'But why not? The bird wants me to stroke him,' said one of the children, a rather sweet little girl of no more than five or six years old.

'Well, if you do he'll nip you on the finger and make you cry,' I said.

'No,' she said disbelievingly. 'He wouldn't do that. He's a nice bird.'

'He will, I promise,' I said. 'And he'll have a good laugh about it too.'

Reluctantly, she listened to me and removed her hand,

although, from the look on her face, she still didn't quite believe me.

Moving on, we approached the catteries and kennels, always a firm favourite with the children. Here, I'd stuck up some notices warning people not to open the cage doors unless they had permission from a member of the RSPCA staff. Again this didn't go down well with the children.

'Why can't we go in and stroke the pussy-cats?' the little girl asked.

'Well,' I said, 'you can if a member of staff lets you in and goes with you, but you can't just let yourself in.'

With our children long grown up, I'd forgotten how persistent a child's questioning can be.

'But why?'

I decided that honesty was the best policy. 'Because once at an open day someone opened a cage door and a cat got so frightened that it ran away from the centre,' I said.

This seemed to satisfy the little girl, for a moment at least. But it wasn't long before she was back on the offensive. 'So why won't you take me in so I can stroke the little kittens?'

I give up, I chuckled to myself, carefully opening the door and ushering in the little girl and the other children and allowing them to interact with the cats for ten minutes.

If ever I felt mildly frustrated by the demands people made at the open day, or indeed at any other time, however, I had learned long ago to bite my tongue. For a start, we were a publicly funded charitable organisation, so people were fully entitled to see what we were doing with their money, within reason of course. Secondly, with young people in particular it was important to educate them about animal welfare. First-hand encounters with animals like these were invaluable in getting our message across. Last, and far from least, however, I had learned that a little kindness towards the more difficult customers could produce the most surprising outcomes.

A few years back, around when we were planning our first open day, I struck up a relationship with an elderly lady who lived in the nearby village of Bolingey. She would get the bus that passed by on the upper road and pop into the centre on a regular basis, always with some kind of pretence regarding an animal problem.

She wasn't the easiest of people to get along with and was highly opinionated. Her conversation was always peppered with comments like 'Why have you put that cat in this pen?' or 'Why don't you put that dog in a bigger kennel?' Once, she even had the cheek to moan that the biscuit we'd served her with a cup of tea was stale. In truth, I think she was just lonely and in search of company. I rather enjoyed the feisty conversations we had.

One day, shortly before the inaugural open day, I happened to be in the village store in Bolingey when I overheard the lady deep in conversation with a friend.

She hadn't seen me, so, positioning myself behind one of the aisles, I eavesdropped for a moment.

'I think it's disgusting they haven't laid on any transport for senior citizens to visit the place,' I heard her say.

'Terrible, isn't it?' her friend concurred.

'They just don't care about us,' she added. 'We're not important enough for them.'

Right, I thought to myself. We'll see about this.

So on the Saturday morning of the open day I hopped in our car and drove to the old lady's house. When I knocked on the door and she answered, the look on her face was a picture.

'Oh, Mr Harper. What a surprise. What do you want?' she said.

'Aren't you ready?' I countered. 'I've come to give you your lift to the open day.'

'My lift, but—'

'Yes, I gather you've been saying you wanted a lift there, so I've got your own personal taxi outside. I'll wait in the car.'

For the first time since I'd met her she was speechless. In the car driving over to the centre she barely said a word. The silence was only temporary, however. Once she was installed at the centre, with a cup of tea and a biscuit in her hand, she grumbled and moaned away all morning, complaining about the crowds, the chairs, the food, the animals. I took it all with a pinch of salt. Secretly, I knew she was having a great time, chatting to familiar faces and sharing whatever local gossip was flying around. She had been one of the very last people to leave when the event came to an end. I'd had to run her home as well, of course.

After that she became a regular visitor to the open days; indeed, they didn't seem quite the same when, a few years later, ill health prevented her from joining us each May or June.

One day, I received a letter from a firm of solicitors. I'd known that the lady had passed away and had been to her funeral in Truro. The letter explained that she had left her entire estate to the local RSPCA, and had asked that I be informed of this. The amount of money involved was substantial, many thousands of pounds.

I was always surprised by the number of people who attended our open days, but this year, perhaps because of the wonderful weather, there were more than ever. By lunchtime the centre was overflowing with visitors. In the field, a couple of inspectors were having to guide people into the few available spaces left in the car park.

Over at the refreshments stall, I could see the ladies from the RSPCA committee handing out cups of tea, coffee and of course lemonade on a more or less continuous basis. Clearly the supplies of the latter had stood up to the test. Well done, Julie, I thought to myself. I was entertaining the idea of having one myself when I saw a familiar face approaching me.

'Hello, Mr Harper. Remember me? I'm the boy who found the buzzard in the bus shelter,' the young lad said.

'Yes, of course. Ronnie, isn't it? Come to see Fury, have you?'

'Please,' he said, beaming.

'Actually, your timing's rather good. He's about due a feed.'

The little buzzard had been faring well since arriving at the centre. Fury hadn't suffered any major injury and simply needed building up. Feeding a very young bird like this is something of a specialist skill. Buzzards, like other birds of prey, can live on a simple diet of day-old chicks. We always kept a good stock of them in the deep-freeze, thanks largely to a poultry farm in Devon, which supplied them to us.

Often, newly arrived birds of prey are reluctant to accept food, so you have to cut the meat up into tiny, softened pieces and offer them with a pair of tweezers. Even so, many birds are hesitant to accept food from this strange source and don't take the meat easily. In this case, the trick is to drag or knock the meat gently against the bird's beak until it snaps at it, out of annoyance as much as anything else.

There had been no need for this with Fury, however. He had obviously been without food for some time and from the first day snatched at the meat immediately it was offered to him. By now, however, I was feeding him differently. I put some meat on the tweezers, then fed it through a hole in the top of the cardboard box where he was sleeping.

'Why are you doing that, Mr Harper?' Ronnie asked.

'Well, I'm trying to make sure he doesn't associate humans with food.'

'Why not?'

'Because once a young wild bird becomes humanised, it will have little chance of surviving in the wild. It will be used to being looked after and won't be able to fend for itself.'

'Oh, I see,' Ronnie said, fascinated.

'Here, do you want to have a go? Just carry a small piece of the meat from the plate in through the hole and wait until you feel the pull of Fury's beak.'

Delighted, Ronnie placed some meat on the tweezers and placed it in the hole. Moments later, when he removed it, the meat was gone. 'There – gone,' he said. 'So what will happen in the next couple of weeks, Mr Harper?' he asked.

'Well, Fury will grow and learn to feed himself. The brown feathers will start to show on his back, and the quills that will become his flight feathers will push through on his wings. In about a month's time he will be fully feathered and I'll put him outside in an aviary, so he can start to do exercises.'

'And after that?'

'And after that I will take him to a falconer friend of mine to make sure he can fly properly. If he can, I will take him up on to a tor on Bodmin Moor and release him into the wild.'

'Good,' Ronnie said, smiling. 'That's where he belongs.'

As we emerged from the treatment room, I saw that

the crowds were thinning and a steady stream of cars were now leaving the car park. The open day was drawing to a close. I was just congratulating myself on what had clearly been a huge success when I saw a couple of people emerging from the yard near the house and laughing loudly.

'Didn't think you saw that kind of thing here,' the giggling young woman said.

'Must be the heat,' the man said.

What's tickled their fancy? I asked myself, after saying goodbye to Ronnie, whose parents were waving for him to join them in leaving. Turning the corner, the answer to my question was soon clear.

There, in the middle of the yard, my collie, Moss, was mounted on top of another dog, with which he was frantically mating. I recognised the other dog as a bitch that had been in the largest kennel and had come into heat in the past few days. I'd of course stuck a notice up warning people not to open the door, but clearly this had been in vain. Some bright spark had let the dog loose.

Fortunately, the two dogs hadn't become tied yet, so I marched over and separated them, which didn't please Moss too much. After sending Moss back to the house, however, I was horrified to discover a little girl standing on the edge of the yard, from where she'd clearly been watching the two amorous dogs in action.

'Excuse me,' she said, 'what were those dogs doing to each other?'

The little girl couldn't have been more than five, and I didn't think it was up to me to introduce her to the concept of the birds and the bees. 'Oh, nothing to worry about,' I said, leading her away to the main area, where I hoped her parents would reclaim her.

'Were they fighting?' she persisted.

'No, they weren't fighting. They were only having a little argument,' I said reassuringly.

It would be nothing compared to the argument I would have if I ever found out who had left the kennel door open.

CHAPTER TEN

Titch

The smallholding lay in the shadow of Bodmin Moor and, as the inspector and I pulled into its yard soon after dawn, was still largely shrouded in darkness. Scanning the property, I could see no obvious signs of life. No lights were visible inside the house; no smoke was rising from its chimneys. In the lee of some large oaks, a row of three run-down wooden outbuildings were shuttered up, seemingly empty. The only vehicle in the yard was a battered old pickup that had had its four tyres removed and was balancing precariously on a pile of concrete blocks. Everything pointed to the premises having been uninhabited for some time, but we had to check it out nevertheless.

The previous evening we had taken a call from someone who lived near the smallholding. Passing by at various times during the past week or so, he had heard muffled barks and cries emanating from the outbuildings.

There had been no sightings of the tenants of the small-holding for some time. They were relatively recent arrivals from 'up country' with little experience of farming. The neighbour feared the strain of running the smallholding had proved too much for them and they had done a midnight flit, leaving their livestock untended and suffering. We had headed off at daybreak this morning to investigate.

Climbing out of the van, the inspector and I were greeted at first by an eerie silence. It wasn't long, however, before we heard a faint banging sound coming from the direction of the outbuildings.

'Sounds like something's trying to let us know it's there,' I said, heading towards the ramshackle sheds.

The banging was coming from the largest of the outbuildings. The door was old and had clearly not been opened for some time. The pair of us began tugging at its handles in an attempt to free it. We were soon regretting it. After a few hefty heaves, the door finally loosened itself and we felt a force pushing with us from within. We watched as part of the door was splintered open by an animal trying to batter its way free. As the door flung open, we both instinctively jumped to one side. It was fortunate that we did. If we hadn't, we would have been flattened by the charging billy goat that suddenly exploded from the darkness, flailing its large and rather dangerous-looking horns. The goat had clearly been deprived of food for a long time because it had quickly forgotten us and was rushing towards an open area of grassland a few yards away. To our relief, it was soon munching away furiously.

As it turned out, the goat seemed to be the only occupant of this outbuilding, which contained nothing more than a rusting pile of motor parts and spare tyres, so we headed to check out a shed nearby. Heaving the doors open – a little more carefully this time – we were greeted by a flock of half-starved hens and ducks. Again they were all in a hurry to get out. In their case, they seemed more interested in drink than food and scuttled their way over to a nearby pig trough, which was half full with muddy rainwater.

'Ruddy idiots,' the inspector said, shaking his head as he watched the poultry slake their thirst. 'Why do these people come down here thinking running a farm is such a piece of cake, Rex?'

'Don't know,' I said. 'I wish they wouldn't, though. Come on, let's take a look at this last shed. See what they've left behind in there.'

The third and final outbuilding was the smallest and least hospitable-looking. It had only a small window, and its roof looked as if it had seen far better days. As we approached, I thought I heard the gentlest of whimpering sounds coming from inside. 'Can you hear that?' I asked the inspector.

'I can. Don't like the sound of it either.'

In contrast to the occupants of the first two buildings, the inmates of the third shed were in no hurry to meet their liberators. When we slid the door open and stepped in, we were aware of a shape scurrying its way into the darkest corner of the building. There was no obvious light source, so we both switched on our torches. The sight we discovered in the corner was one that neither of us would forget in a hurry.

Lying in the corner were five puppies. They were terrier crosses of some kind, by my estimate about ten weeks old. Each one was horribly emaciated and listless, and each was extremely nervous. As we moved towards what seemed to be their den, they all retreated towards an area covered in faeces. Moving closer, I also made out the shape of a dead dog, presumably the puppies' unfortunate mother. The obvious explanation was that she had died trying to keep her litter alive, sacrificing herself for the sake of her offspring. Shining my torch along the side of the dog's body, I could see that the puppies had even begun to eat away at the carcass. She had made the ultimate sacrifice and allowed her puppies to cannibalise her. It was a pathetic sight.

As I dropped to my knees in an attempt to persuade one of the puppies to come to me, I noticed the mother's head twitch ever so slightly. At first I didn't believe my eyes and ignored the movement, but the inspector had spotted it too. 'Good God, she's alive,' he said.

'Can't be,' I said.

'She is. Why don't you see if you can do anything for her while I gather up the puppies?'

When I moved in to look more closely at the dog, I saw that she was in the most horrendous state, barely clinging to life. She was breathing spasmodically, twitching as if in pain, and her eyes were flickering erratically. Inspecting her body, I saw that her puppies had inflicted large, gaping wounds along her side and back. The young dogs had eaten away so much flesh in one area that the mother's spine was exposed. I really wasn't sure if she was strong enough to be moved, let alone whether she would survive a journey in the van. I had to try, however. There was no option.

It wasn't long before the inspector had successfully gathered the five pups and safely installed them in a cage in the back of the van. He then helped me shift the mother. As we lifted her off the ground, she let out a loud whimper. When we lay her on a blanket on the back of the van, she made an awful gurgling sound, as if she was drawing her last breath. I really didn't think she would last a journey of any distance.

I asked the inspector to take me and the dog straight to a vet, fully expecting to find our passenger dead on arrival, another victim of human fecklessness and cruelty.

Calls to abandoned premises like this were unfortunately a far-too-common occurrence. In recent times it seemed like more and more people were being tempted to move from the more populous towns and cities of the UK to enjoy what they hoped would be a rural idyll in the Cornish countryside. Once established here, they would set themselves up in a smallholding or farm and surround themselves with animals that they were completely incapable of keeping properly. It was left to the RSPCA and the county's other animal charities to pick up the pieces when it inevitably went wrong.

I'd been involved in a similar – though less horrific –

case to this one the previous year. A young married couple had rented a local cottage with a view to starting a new life there. They'd been office workers in London and had traded in their life for a simpler existence, living close to nature. Unfortunately, life proved a little too simple for both of them and they'd soon parted. Quite how they managed it, I never understood, but they moved out, each thinking the other had taken their Dobermann bitch with them. In fact, the dog had been left locked up in the empty cottage, where she'd spent five days before being found by a neighbour, who had been alerted by her howling.

When myself, an RSPCA inspector and the local police broke into the house, we found a scene of complete chaos. The carpets had been chewed, the floorboards ripped up and the back of the front door scored with teeth marks. When we located the Dobermann, she was in an utter fury, growling and baring her teeth at us from the top of the stairs. Anticipating this, I'd come armed with a pair of thick gauntlets and a grasper. When I approached the dog, she made no effort to back off and stood her ground at the top of the stairs. With a flick of the grasper, however, I was able to bring her under control and lead her back to the van.

As was so often the case with aggressive dogs, her whole attitude changed after that. It was as if she was grateful for the human contact. When I got her back to the centre, she calmed down considerably. She spent two weeks with us, becoming a very likeable and obedient dog in the process. We called her Mitzie.

It took the RSPCA and the police two weeks to trace the residents of the cottage. Both claimed to be appalled that the other had left the dog there, but it was the husband who came to collect her.

To judge by the dog's reaction, she had clearly held him in some affection. It made me wonder what had really happened when the two people had split up. Had the wife abandoned the dog out of the desire to exact some kind of sick revenge? When Mitzie was taken to him, she jumped straight into the back of his open-top sports car, wagging her tail and barking happily. As they drove off, we assumed that was the last we'd see of them, but an hour or so later, when Julie and I were in the middle of our lunch, we heard a scratching at the back door. I went to see what it was and, to my amazement, discovered Mitzie wagging her tail and looking extremely pleased to see me.

'What are you doing here, young lady?' I asked.

I soon learned what had happened, when her owner pulled up in his sports car twenty minutes or so later. I'd gone back to the office by now and he arrived there breathing heavily, in a terrible flap.

'Haven't seen my dog, have you?' he said. 'She just jumped out of the car two miles down the road and ran into a field. I've been scouring the fields and lanes but I've had no joy.' He was still jabbering away when Julie appeared in the office doorway, with Mitzie standing alongside her.

'Probably came back to say thank you,' she said, letting the dog loose to return to her grateful owner once more.

Needless to say, the sports car's roof was firmly shut when they resumed their journey.

When Karen summoned me to the phone to talk to the vet a week or so after we'd recovered the animals from the abandoned smallholding, I was certain it was to deliver the inevitable bad news about the poor mother. I was taken aback when he greeted me in a seemingly cheery mood.

'Morning, Rex,' he said. 'Fancy popping over to collect your friend from Bodmin?'

Along with the other recovered animals – including the angry billy goat – the five puppies had responded well to the care they received at the centre, putting on weight and regaining their strength steadily. If I'm honest, though, I'd written the mother off. When I'd last seen her, she had been in such terrible pain that I'd assumed the vet would be unable to do much to keep her alive. She'd also suffered extensive spinal injuries as a result of the wounds the puppies had inflicted. I'd talked it through with the vet and agreed that if she didn't respond to treatment, then she would have to be euthanised. I'd fully expected him to tell me that's what had happened but instead he told me she'd made a remarkable recovery.

'She's made of strong stuff,' he concluded.

'She must be, given the state I found her in,' I said.

I agreed to collect her and headed off to the vet's almost immediately. I found the mother with stitches still visible in her side and back and a splint on her hind leg, which had suffered nerve damage as a result of the spinal injuries. She was still a nervous dog, but her demeanour was 100 per cent better than it had been on that dark morning at the smallholding. It was a minor miracle.

As I drove home, I quickly made a decision about her future. I knew that she was not going to adapt easily to life at the centre kennels. She was still too anxious to fit in with the other dogs, and the severity of her injuries meant that she would never recover well enough to be a suitable candidate for rehoming. So given all this, I'd concluded that there was little choice but to make her the latest member of our extended animal family.

Back at Ferndale, she was soon ensconced in a small kennel at the rear of our garden. Julie was busy in the fields when I arrived, and joined me as I fed the new arrival her first meal.

'Who's this?' she asked.

'This is the poor mother I told you about from Bodmin.'

'Really?' she said, shocked. 'I thought she was beyond all help.'

'It appears not. Seems she's a mother in a million.'

Julie kneeled down and stroked her gently. 'She's a titchy little thing, isn't she?' she said, turning to me with a knowing smile. 'I suppose she's staying with us for a while?' she said.

'I suppose she is,' I agreed, giving the dog a gentle ruffle. 'Aren't you, Titch?'

I shouldn't have been quite so surprised that the dog had recovered, I suppose. Over the years I'd frequently been amazed by the way some animals recovered from the most terrible injuries. Back in the early days, when Julie and I had run a small sanctuary from the garden of our old cottage, the Rosery, we'd been brought a cat that had been rescued from – of all places – the engine of a car.

The vehicle's owner had been visiting Perranporth on holiday and had heard a terrible, sickening crunching noise coming from under the bonnet when he had started his engine. When he'd lifted the bonnet, he'd found the mutilated body of a tabby kitten tangled up in the fan belt. The little animal had been barely alive. Fortunately, a shop owner who witnessed the incident knew that I was working in the nearby post office and ran to fetch me. Even more fortunately, our local vet was in his surgery. In next to no time the pathetic bundle of blood and fur was on his table and being given sedatives by injection to ease the pain.

Two days later the kitten, minus a leg and a tail, was brought to the Rosery, where she remained for many years. Jenny, as we named her, developed a liking for lying outside the front gate on the tarmac road in the sunshine. This was not a good idea of course, but in those days the traffic was very light and when she heard a car approaching she would get up and hobble in her unique way back into the garden. Many was the time when we'd had a knock on the door from a concerned passing motorist to report a severely disabled cat heading towards our front door.

Titch wasn't quite as badly disfigured as Jenny, but it was clear her injuries were going to leave her with permanent disabilities. The most lasting injury was to her hind leg, which, because of the nerve damage, remained stiff and awkward. As a result, she found it difficult moving around and walked with a distinctly lopsided gait. Titch remained wary of strangers and would disappear into the overgrowth near the railway bank at the far end of the fields every now and again. On one occasion she stayed there for a few weeks, only emerging to eat her food in the evenings. Hard as I tried, I couldn't persuade her to break this habit. It took the unlikely friendship she formed with another troubled canine to stop her hiding away like this.

Animals often sense vulnerability and weakness in each other. While this brings out the ruthless side in some, it can bring out the compassionate and caring in others. Julie and I had seen this when we had been caring for Jenny, our cat. She had been looked after by our old terrier bitch, Cindy, a specialist in fostering kittens. When Jenny had arrived with us, wrapped up in bandages, Cindy had curled herself round her protectively, repelling anyone or anything she perceived as being a threat to her patient. The two remained devoted for years.

In the case of Titch, her Good Samaritan was a German shepherd called Kaiser. Kaiser had been brought to us having been removed from a travellers' camp. A passer-by had seen one of the travellers trying to run him over with a lorry and had called in the RSPCA. He had, for understandable reasons, been a very nervous and untrusting dog when he first arrived but, like Mitzie the Dobermann, had calmed down immeasurably.

Titch had disappeared into the overgrowth again and hadn't been seen for a couple of days when, one evening, walking back from the fields, I saw her hobbling alongside Kaiser. Somehow the two had become friends and Kaiser had persuaded the smaller dog to return to the farm. At first I thought they were an odd couple, but as their friendship deepened, I saw that they were in fact kindred spirits. In time, Titch's leg problems improved so that she only had a slight stiffness to her walk. She became a very happy dog, provided she was free to roam the farm, usually with Kaiser at her side.

At one point we found an owner willing to take her in. She was a dedicated dog lover with experience looking after rescue dogs, but within twenty-four hours of Titch leaving us, the lady was on the phone telling us that she was terribly upset, shaking and sitting by the door. According to the lady, Titch had 'tears running down her nose', which I rather doubted. We took her back nevertheless and, much to Kaiser's delight, never tried to send her away from the farm again.

The two dogs remained inseparable for years, until one morning when I discovered Titch curled up alongside Kaiser in the barn. When I approached her, she barked plaintively, as if she was in pain. Looking at Kaiser, I saw that her giant friend and protector had died during the night. Titch had stayed there with him nevertheless.

By then Titch was ailing too. She was nearly blind and was stiff with rheumatism, which had exacerbated the problems she'd had with her legs. I knew she wouldn't last long and would miss Kaiser terribly. So a day or so later I arranged with our vet to have her quietly put to sleep. I buried the two dogs together in the fields where their friendship had blossomed, sad to lose them but happy at the thought of the contentment both had found late in their lives.

CHAPTER ELEVEN

Attack of the Devil Birds

The sun was setting over the coast to the west as I turned the van into the centre at the end of another busy day. I found Karen and Sue in the office, finishing off the day's paperwork and chatting to one of the inspectors.

'Have a look in the cleaning unit, Rex,' Karen said, turning to me as I dropped the keys to the van on the desk.

'Why? What's there?'

'Just take a look, Rex,' Karen said again. 'See what turned up today.'

I headed out to the unit intrigued but mildly worried. At this time of the year the cleaning unit was relatively quiet. There had been no storms or heavy weather of any kind. Surely we didn't have an influx of oiled birds again. I opened the door carefully, not quite sure what to expect. As I stepped inside, I was greeted by a loud croak.

Standing at the other end of the unit was a large cormorant. With their long snakelike necks and bright-green eyes, there is a strange, almost prehistoric-looking quality to this, one of the most distinctive-looking of seabirds. It is little wonder the cormorant's nickname is the 'devil bird'. It really does look quite demonic.

The seabird unit was about thirty feet long and was fitted out with sinks, for washing and cleaning our oiled patients, and a series of collapsible pens, which we erected as and when they were needed. None was up at the moment so the cormorant had virtually the whole space to itself.

Looking at the bird more closely, I could see why it had been brought in. It was standing at the far end of the building with a yard or so of nylon fishing line trailing behind it. My guess was that it had caught a fish that had already been hooked, swallowed it and then got itself tangled up in the line. It had obviously panicked and tried to untangle itself but only succeeded in making matters worse. The line was now tightly coiled round its wings and legs.

'So what do you think of our new guest, then?' a voice said from behind me. It was Karen.

'Evil-looking creatures, aren't they? No wonder they call them devil birds. Where did he come in from?'

'One of the lakes over by Newquay,' she said. 'Someone was fishing and saw the bird caught up on the end of his line. The owner of the lake called and we brought him in. Apparently he was a real handful.'

'I bet,' I said, casting an eye over the cormorant, who

was still croaking away at the far end of the unit. 'Better leave me to it.'

Cormorants normally live on the coast but sometimes build their untidy nests in trees, usually close to rivers or the sea itself. They are curiously ill-equipped to spend long amounts of time in the water. The cormorant's plumage isn't completely waterproof, so its feathers can only take a certain amount of immersion before getting waterlogged. As a result, fishing cormorants leave the water before this happens. It is why you see so many of them standing on posts or trees with their wings widespread to the wind and sun. It is their way of drying off before the next fishing trip.

I decided to take a closer look, but as I walked towards the big bird, it started to croak more loudly. To my surprise, it then lunged at me with its long hooked beak. It was obviously intent on attacking but, fortunately, was handicapped by the line wrapped round its legs. I knew if it caught me, it was capable of delivering a nasty bite and would twist my flesh with its strong hooked beak, so I didn't want to take any risks. When I moved away, the bird lurched forwards again. As it struggled to reach me, it was glaring menacingly with those devilish green eyes.

I'm sure it would have carried on, but at this point the nylon twisted round its legs became even more restricting. Suddenly the cormorant started to lose its balance. It wobbled briefly, then fell over on to its side, croaking angrily as it did so. Oh, well, this might be my chance, I said to myself.

I ran to the storeroom nearby and gathered up a

blanket and a sharp pair of scissors. I quickly got back to the unit, where I found the still-furious cormorant writhing on the floor. The first thing I needed to do was demobilise its rather dangerous beak, so I wrapped the blanket round the bird, being careful to cover its beak. I then carefully cut away the tangled nylon line, which had started to cut into the bird's legs. Once the legs were freed, I went to work on its wings. I didn't want to stress the bird out too much, but as I cleared the last bits of line from its wings it seemed remarkably relaxed. It also seemed very tired, for understandable reasons. I decided to let the bird rest a bit before attempting the more difficult job of examining its throat, where, in all likelihood, the fishing hook was still lodged. But no sooner had I freed it from the blanket than it was up on its feet croaking angrily once more. With its wings raised, it attacked me again, this time chasing me down the whole length of the building. I beat a hasty retreat.

That wasn't the first time I'd been attacked by a bird, far from it. I'd learned long ago that when you work with animals there are times when they don't respond in the way you expect. I always remember a time when I went to Bristol Zoo as a young boy growing up in Bath. I was a fairly regular visitor there and had made friends with some of the keepers. On this particular occasion I wandered behind the fences to find a friend I knew worked in one of the aviaries. I was walking along when I was suddenly aware of something behind me. Before I could turn round, it had grabbed me round the waist and put me in a vice-like grip. For a moment I was mildly panicked. 'What the heck,' I shouted. I was astonished when I managed to spin round and see it was a pelican. I had seen the bird around. It was the only one of its kind in the zoo at the time and stood out, but I'd had no idea it was capable of attacking people like this.

I managed to turn my body so that I could get a grip on its enormous and extremely powerful beak. It took a real effort to prise it open long enough for me to break free. Even when I did manage to release myself and run off towards the bird keepers' quarters, the pelican didn't give up. It waddled behind me, grunting crossly to itself all the way.

Although alarming, it was an experience that came in handy a few years later, when I became a postman in Cornwall. Encounters like the one I'd had with the pelican had taught me to be careful of all animals, no matter how docile they may appear. So when I learned about a Chinese gander that had been terrorising postmen, I knew to take the threat seriously.

Geese are renowned for their protective nature, and ganders can become especially aggressive during the breeding season. This particular gander lived in an orchard attached to a small cottage with his harem of geese. If an intruder strayed into his territory, the gander would attack from the rear, running up behind his hapless victim with lowered head and grabbing a leg with his beak. He would then hold on tightly, twisting whatever skin or material he could. I'd heard talk of this gander in the sorting office, so when I was given the round that included his cottage, I was ready for him.

I'd barely got a dozen yards up the cottage's garden path when I heard his large webbed feet pattering up behind me. Turning round just as the gander was about to make a lunge for my rear, I beat him to it and grabbed hold of his neck. I then lifted him off his feet and shook him. The gander was horrified. When I put him down, he stretched his neck as high as he could and waddled off haughtily, beak pointing skywards, calling me every name he could think of. Probably in Chinese.

The following morning I told the other postmen what to do if the gander decided to try it on with them. The advice proved useful when the gander did indeed attack again. The victim did as I had told him, turning at the last minute to grab the bird's neck. However, as he did so, his postbag slipped off his shoulder and the strap went over the gander's head. This completely fazed the gander, who now found himself saddled with a bag of letters round his neck. He shuffled around the orchard until at last he managed to rid himself of the encumbrance and returned, shaken, to the company of his wives. That was the last time the gander attacked. From then on he contented himself with adopting a threatening posture and shouting Chinese obscenities at visitors from a safe distance.

By far the feistiest bird I ever encountered, however, was the large turkey that we'd kept on the farm for a few years when we'd first arrived at Ferndale. Male, or cock, turkeys are impressive-looking creatures at the best of times, but this one, an American bronze turkey, really was a sight to behold. He would strut around the yard with his tail spread out like a fan, challenging anyone or anything to try to assert their authority over him. No one did, mainly because he had the most ferocious temper. When something annoyed him, which was quite often, his wattles and head would turn bright red and he would charge at the culprit.

At first other poultry were the main targets for his anger, but as he became more confident, dogs and even humans became fair game. He would charge at them if he thought they were infringing on his territory. Needless to say, the more successful he was, the bigger his territory became.

At the time the girls who worked at the RSPCA centre had to cross our farmyard to get to work. I lost count of the number of times the day would begin with screams of 'Rex, get this bloody turkey out of the way.' On one occasion I ran out of the house to find two of the girls, Sue and Liz, perched precariously on top of a gate, desperately trying to avoid the gobbling turkey's beak as he tried to nip their legs. Even Julie and my youngest children, Zoe and Klair, had to run the gauntlet of the turkey some days.

I used to find the whole thing hilarious, until, that was, I became the turkey's latest victim. I was unloading the van one morning when, completely out of the blue, I felt something ramming into me at speed. The force of the collision propelled me forwards into the back of the van, sending my feet into the air. The next thing I knew I was being nipped ferociously on the legs.

Julie appeared from the house during the midst of the attack and was still laughing uproariously when I finally chased the turkey back to the other side of the yard. 'Not so funny when you're on the receiving end, is it?' she laughed.

Needless to say, the bird didn't stay with us for long after that. A large turkey turned up in the deep-freeze a few days later, an early contribution to that year's Christmas dinner.

Ever since then, I'd made it a policy to ensure that no animal got the upper hand. So the morning after my run-in with the cormorant, I got up determined to finish off what I'd started. I went into the storeroom and equipped myself once more with a blanket and scissors, plus a pair of thick gloves. I also decided I needed an assistant. I wasn't going to leave anything to chance and get bitten again.

'Right,' I said, walking into the office to find the girls already there. 'Who is going to come and help me sort out our awkward customer? I need someone to hold our friend while I check out its throat.'

Vicky volunteered immediately.

'Seconds out, round two,' I said with a wink to her as we prepared to enter the unit moments later.

After a night's rest, the cormorant seemed as angry as ever. It was croaking away again in the corner of the unit. I decided it was time to act decisively. We wasted no time in wrapping the cormorant up in the blanket.

'Keep its beak shut,' I told Vicky.

With the bird immobilised, I carefully felt along its

neck to see if I could locate the fish hook. It didn't take long. I soon found a sharp object lodged in the bird's throat. It felt fairly large, and had come to rest in the loose skin. As Vicky held the cormorant's beak shut, I tried to find the back of the hook. Having done so, I angled it so that the point was facing me, just as I had done with the kingfisher. It was then a simple matter to push the point through the bird's skin and withdraw the whole hook with its attached nylon line. A few moments later, with the line cut, I was able to draw it back and out through the bird's beak.

'There. Perhaps he won't be quite so aggressive now,' I said to Vicky.

The bird must have been in considerable discomfort. Happily, however, it seemed to be easing already. The cormorant flapped its wings and waddled off into the far corner of the unit. Its days with us would soon come to an end, I felt sure. I, for one, wasn't going to miss him.

CHAPTER TWELVE

Miss Loveday

Experience had taught Julie and me a great deal since we'd started looking after animals almost thirty years earlier. We knew now, for instance, that it was imperative to check the home of prospective owners of animals. We also knew that this had to be done, regardless of how perfect, charming or well intentioned the potential owner might seem when they visited us at the centre. The truth of the matter was that things were not always what they seemed. And if any of us ever felt ourselves forgetting that, all we had to do was remember one of the most extraordinary people we had dealt with over the years, Miss Loveday.

She'd come into our lives a few years after we'd opened the centre at Ferndale. I'd been walking up the hill one morning, after taking a couple of our canine inmates for a walk down the lane, when I'd discovered a figure in the middle of the road outside the centre. As I drew closer, I saw she was a rather frail-looking lady, dressed in a somewhat threadbare overcoat. She appeared hesitant and a little confused. To be honest, she looked lost.

'Can I help you?' I asked.

'Oh, well, yes, I hope so,' she said, perking up slightly at the sight of me and the two lively dogs on the end of my twin leash. 'I wanted to talk to someone about finding myself a dog. Looks like it might be you.'

'Looks like it might be.' I smiled. 'Come with me and we'll sort you out with a cup of tea.'

Karen and Sue were soon sitting her down in the office and offering her tea and sympathy. Between sips, she explained that her name was Miss Loveday and she had walked all the way from Perranporth, two miles away, after catching a bus from Truro, eight miles before that.

'Goodness me, no wonder you look so tired. You must be keen on finding a dog,' I said.

'Well, yes, I am rather,' she said, smiling. 'I'm looking for a little companion really.'

When she'd recovered her strength a little, I took her by the arm and led her out to the pens. There, she cast her eye over the dozen or so small dogs we had in residence.

'Oh, he's rather lovely,' she said, fairly quickly latching on to a pretty but rather mischievous-looking cross-bred Yorkshire terrier. 'What's his name?'

'Well, he doesn't really have one.'

'Oh, right. He looks like a naughty chap. If I could have him, I'd call him Scamp.'

I saw no reason why she couldn't start the adoption

process immediately. She seemed like an ideal owner and Scamp, as he was now known, had spent enough time at the centre for us to be confident he was ready to go to a new home. We were soon doing the paperwork, legally installing Miss Loveday as the new owner.

'Where do you live, Miss Loveday?'

'Number twelve Stanley Avenue, Truro,' she said.

There was something about the little old lady that brought out the protective side in me, so I offered to drive her back to Perranporth to catch the bus to Truro. She accepted happily and we chatted away during the short drive. Her mood was transformed from earlier in the day. A few minutes later I watched her leaving on the bus with little Scamp happily nestling on her lap. I felt like we'd found the dog a really good home. It looked like a match made in heaven.

I was pleasantly surprised when, a few weeks later, Miss Loveday reappeared. Once more she had walked to us from Perranporth.

'I've come to find a friend for Scamp,' she told us, smiling. 'You were so good to me last time I thought I'd come here first.'

Once more we all fussed over her, and once more we found her what seemed like an ideal dog, this time a Cairn terrier bitch, whom we knew was called Candy. Once again I transported the pair to the bus for Truro and waved them on their way.

I forgot all about Miss Loveday for a few months. It was only when I visited Truro one morning a few months later that she popped back into mind. I was about to climb into the van when I saw a lady walking towards me with a small Cairn terrier bitch. I have a very good memory for dogs, if not their owners, and I was certain that I recognised her.

'Excuse me,' I said to the lady. 'Sorry to bother you, but is that Candy?'

The lady was very surprised at first, but then pleased that her dog had been recognised in the street. 'Well, she used to be called Candy,' she told me, 'but when we bought her we changed her name. She's called Bella now.'

I was in my RSPCA uniform, but I explained to her who I was in any case. 'Did you by any chance acquire her from a lady called Miss Loveday?' I asked.

The lady's face suddenly took on a rather emotional look. 'Yes, poor Miss Loveday,' she said.

'Oh, dear,' I said, fearing the worst. 'Is she all right?'

'Well, yes, in herself she's all right,' she said. 'But she's fallen on hard times, I think, poor soul. She told us she couldn't afford to keep Bella, or Candy as she was. We made sure we gave her a good price. It was a fair bit of money for us, but we don't regret it – she's such a sweet dog.'

I didn't let my face betray what I was thinking. 'Well, I'm certain she's found a good home,' I said, before heading back to the van.

Once I was safely in the van, I couldn't help shaking my head. When a member of the public took a cat, dog or indeed any other animal from us, they generally made only a small cash donation, mainly to cover our expenses.

As far as the RSPCA was concerned, these owners were undertaking to look after creatures that had been given a raw deal in life. We didn't want to charge them large amounts of money. Equally, however, we didn't expect people to profit from the animal's adoption, certainly not at the speed with which Miss Loveday had cashed in Candy, and presumably Scamp too. This was simply not on.

Who'd have thought a little old lady like that could be so devious? I wondered to myself. I bet she's selling all sorts of dogs around the county.

Back at the office, my suspicions were quickly confirmed. I called a couple of dog sanctuaries I knew – one in Newquay, the other on the south coast, near Falmouth. The Falmouth one did mention having trouble with a woman who'd repeatedly taken dogs from there, but my description didn't quite ring true to the manager.

I didn't do anything about it immediately. Instead I decided to wait and see if Miss Loveday appeared again. Sure enough, a couple of weeks later she reappeared at the centre, in her usual breathless, slightly bedraggled state. This time, however, I was ready for her.

'Sorry, Miss Loveday,' I said, placing a cup of tea in front of her, 'but you've made a wasted journey today. We don't have any small dogs suitable for you. In fact, we've got no dogs ready to leave here at all.'

'Oh, dear, what a pity,' she said, sipping her tea.

'But I'll tell you what, I'm going into Truro now. Why don't I give you a lift and drop you off at home? I'd love to see how Scamp and Candy are getting on.'

Miss Loveday did not seem too pleased at this suggestion, but I insisted and off we went in the van, heading towards Stanley Avenue, the address she'd given us on both the registration forms. When we arrived in Truro, I asked Miss Loveday for directions but a vague look came on to her face. 'You are going to think I'm awful, Mr Harper,' she said, 'but I've clean forgotten the way from here.'

This completely took me aback. For a few moments I felt terrible. Was the woman sick? Had she got some kind of memory loss? I didn't want to take any undue risks, so after a short while I decided to take her to the police station, where perhaps she would be recognised.

As it turned out, the police car park was quite full, so I dropped Miss Loveday off, telling her to go to the reception area and that I would join her as soon as I had parked the van. When I finally made it into the station five minutes or so later, there was no sign of my passenger.

The officer behind the reception desk hadn't seen her. 'No, haven't seen anyone matching that description,' he said, looking at me as if I was slightly unhinged.

I must have appeared shocked. 'Well, this is extraordinary,' I said to the policeman, before explaining what had been going on. 'Look, here's the address,' I said, handing over a piece of paper she'd filled in when she'd adopted Scamp.

The policeman took a quick look at the address. 'Hmm. It seems your mystery deepens,' he said.

'Why? What do you mean?' I said.

'There's no Stanley Avenue in Truro.'

I headed back to the centre feeling deflated, defeated and a little bit silly. By now I felt pretty certain that the whole episode had been a con from the start. I had been taken for a mug by a little lady who didn't look as if butter would melt in her mouth.

When I got back to the centre, I discovered Karen, Sue and Les, the chief inspector, sitting around having a tea break. Pouring myself a mug, I rather shamefacedly told them what had happened.

'Comes to something when you start losing old ladies as well as two dogs,' laughed Les. 'You must be slipping, mate.'

'Glad to be providing some amusement,' I said, feeling sorry for myself.

Les asked me to talk him through the whole thing. As I did so, he suddenly stopped me. 'I know this lady,' he said. 'I had to go and call on her once – nothing serious, just a nosy-neighbour complaint. She lives in Falmouth, not Truro. Shall we go and pay her a visit?'

'Wild horses couldn't keep me from coming, Les. You drive.'

It took us the best part of an hour to get to Falmouth. Once there, we drove to a long line of terraced houses, all with steps leading down to basement areas and flats.

'I'm sure she lives along here somewhere,' said Les.

We were approaching the end of the terrace when Les suddenly hit the brakes and pointed to the pavement ahead of us. 'There she is.'

Sure enough, there was Miss Loveday, shopping bag in

one hand, walking away from us down the street. As we drew into the kerb alongside Miss Loveday, she turned and obviously spotted the RSPCA van. She walked hurriedly towards one of the nearby basement steps, scurried down them and vanished through a door.

Les and I jumped out of the van and, feeling a little bit like we'd stepped into a scene from a police show on television, started chasing her. When we got to the door, which she had left partly open, there was no sign of her apart from the shopping bag, which now lay on the floor. The door opened into a long passage. On one side was a small flat, which appeared to be empty – certainly there was no barking to indicate that a dog was in residence. At the far end of the passage was another door, again partly open, and beyond that an overgrown garden with a gate leading out on to a maze of lanes.

'Looks like she's done a runner,' I said to Les.

'Well, now that she realises we know where she lives and what she has been up to, it might put her off trying to get any more dogs under false pretences,' Les agreed. 'Come on, let's get back.'

At the office, I contacted all the people I knew who were involved with dog rescue, warning them to be on their guard in case Miss Loveday visited them. No one did encounter her again. Unless, of course, she was wearing a disguise, which, given her resourcefulness, wouldn't have surprised me one jot.

CHAPTER THIRTEEN

An Eagle in the Airing Cupboard

'Morning, Rex. Any chance you could give me a hand collecting something off the London train later on? I think it will interest you.'

The voice on the other end of the telephone line was a familiar one: Peter, a fellow bird enthusiast and falconer, who kept a number of birds of prey near Perranporth. Peter went on to explain that the previous night he'd got a call from someone at Heathrow Airport. A rare South American forest eagle, a harpy, had arrived in London in transit by plane from its home in Bolivia to a large zoo somewhere on the Continent.

'Apparently a partition in the hold of the plane collapsed and the crate was crushed,' he explained. 'They think the harpy was badly injured. They've sedated him and put him on the train for me to pick up at Truro. I'm going to see if I can get him on the mend.'

I knew only a little about this bird; the main thing I'd

read was that harpies are incredibly skilled predators. In their natural environment, the rainforests of South America, they weave their way around under the canopy of trees like deadly stealth bombers, snatching unsuspecting sloths and even quite large monkeys clean off their branches. My curiosity was definitely aroused.

Things were pretty quiet at the office, so I agreed to travel to Truro in the van with Peter. We pulled up in the car park a few minutes after the London train had left for its onward journey to Penzance and headed straight for the parcel office where Peter had been told to collect his unusual delivery.

We walked in to find two guards talking to a third guard who was sitting in a chair looking rather shaken. His face was drained, as if he'd seen a ghost. The most senior of the guards saw us arrive and – probably noticing my RSPCA overalls – turned to me. 'Are you the animal fellas?' he said. We both nodded. 'Good. About time you came to collect this bleedin' dog of yours.'

'Dog?' Peter and I said in unison.

'Yes. I don't know what flamin' breed it is. It's definitely not one we've ever seen. The damned thing scared the living daylights out of Dave here,' he said, pointing at his ashen-faced colleague.

'What do you mean?' I asked, looking at the man.

'I was putting the crate away when something came out of a crack in the side of it,' Dave stuttered.

'Something? What exactly?'

'It was like a dragon's foot. It had claws and scales on it, and it was flailing around trying to cut itself out of there. It's the weirdest-looking thing I've ever seen.'

Peter and I avoided looking at each other because we knew we'd burst out laughing if we made eye contact.

'Well, I've got no idea who told you it was a dog, because it's not,' Peter said.

'Oh,' said the chief guard. 'What is it, then?'

'It's a giant South American eagle.'

'What?' all three guards said at once.

'What the hell are they doing sticking that on a train to Truro?' said Dave.

Peter went on to explain what had happened during the bird's journey across the world and how he was going to help him recuperate over in Perranporth.

'Sooner you than me, mate,' Dave said, shaking his head.

'So how come we weren't told what it was, then?' the senior guard said, looking through a sheaf of paperwork. 'I'm sure it said it was a dog.'

'I've no idea,' Peter said with a shrug of his shoulders.

I could see things might get a bit bogged down here, so I looked at my watch and interrupted. 'Time's getting on, Peter. I've got to get back to the RSPCA centre.'

'Yes, best thing is if we take this animal off your hands right away,' Peter said gratefully, turning to the senior guard.

'Dave, you show them where your friend is,' he said, pointing the way towards a doorway in the far corner.

'It's in the stockroom over here,' Dave said. 'But don't expect me to help you shift it. I'm not going near that bleedin' thing again.'

We found a large crate standing on a table in the corner of the room. It had collected a number of stickers and markings on its long journey and was covered in Spanish and English notes saying, 'Fragile', 'Animal in Transit' and 'Handle With Care'.

It wasn't hard to detect where the crate had been damaged. One side looked squashed and battered, and the crushing motion had opened a large crack that ran across one corner at an angle. There was no sign of anything protruding from the crack, but there were odd scratching and shuffling sounds coming from inside the container.

'Sounds like he might be waking up,' I said.

'OK. Heave ho,' Peter said, as we positioned ourselves either side of the container. 'Better get this chap out of here before he frightens any more of the natives.'

As we carried the box through the car park, the odd noises emanating from inside the crate drew curious glances from passers-by. One young boy asked us what we had in the box. 'Oh, just a dog,' I said, seeing no cause to alarm any more of Truro's good citizens.

Peter and I breathed a sigh of relief when we shut the doors of the van and headed off towards his house in Perranporth, half an hour away.

The creature that revealed itself when we stripped down the crate was one of the strangest I'd ever set eyes on. The harpy had a thickset body that was brown at the back, pale on the breast and had a circular ruff of black feathers round the neck. He had a short tail and a crest behind his head, which raised up when the bird was excited or felt threatened.

The bird's most impressive features, however, were his beak and talons. The beak was large, black, hooked and appeared deadly. The legs were powerful and scaled and led to large toes that were attached to a fearsome-looking set of razor-sharp, downward-curving talons.

'I can see why that poor guard looked so scared,' smiled Peter.

'So can I. Wouldn't fancy being on the receiving end of those,' I added.

We placed the harpy on a large log that Peter had installed in the garage. The bird sat motionless while we looked at him. The eagle was listless and slightly groggy still, but it was clear he was in some kind of pain – and no wonder. Peter and I saw that his right wing was broken quite badly. It was hanging limply at the bird's side, like a shattered branch dangling on a tree.

'That doesn't look good at all,' I said.

'No, it doesn't. I'd guess that's going to have to be amputated.'

I helped Peter install the harpy in a secure cage before heading homewards.

'Keep me posted on its progress,' I said.

'Will do. I'll get an X-ray done tomorrow and see where we go from there,' Peter said as he saw me off.

I regarded myself as a pretty knowledgeable bird expert, but Peter was someone to whom I would often turn for advice. Thanks to him, I had learned a great deal about birds of prey. I'd also had some memorable moments too.

Peter was a keen falconer and over the years I'd spent

many happy hours with him hunting with goshawks and peregrines, usually on the extensive sand dunes at Perranporth. Once, I'd watched Peter use a goshawk to hunt rabbits. He'd confidently predicted that the bird would be able to chase and catch a rabbit before it reached the safety of its burrow. Unfortunately, when a rabbit popped up, it turned out to be a rather large and strong example of the species. The hawk, as Peter had promised, caught the rabbit easily enough, but when it grabbed its back, the animal kept on running at full speed, dragging the unfortunate bird with it. Peter had to recover the hawk from a thick bramble bush, where it had been unceremoniously deposited, minus the rabbit.

On another occasion Peter imported a male Indian peregrine known as a black shaheen, a darker, smaller version of our own peregrine. He had been impatient to take his new acquisition hunting, so one bright autumn morning we walked together over the vast expanse of sand hills looking for suitable quarry. It soon presented itself in the form of a single partridge, which suddenly flew up from between the clumps of marram grass. In a flash the little falcon was after it, but suddenly, like a thunderbolt, a second peregrine swooped with tremendous speed at the two racing birds. Things happened so fast that it was hardly possible to take everything in, but as the partridge dropped like a stone into some lush vegetation on a marshy patch of ground, the little falcon, deprived of his prey, turned on his pursuer, shrieking his displeasure. The two birds of prey appeared to be nothing more than a flying ball of feathers for a few seconds and then both shot into the sky, spiralling and rocketing up until they were mere specks in the blue. Their metallic calls floated down, gradually getting fainter until there were no sounds other than the distant roar of the Atlantic surf and the song of skylarks.

Peter was beside himself. He'd had his new bird a matter of days and he'd already lost him. For an hour or so we waited, combing the heavens with binoculars, but there was no sign of the missing falcon. We agreed to meet back there the following morning in the hope he might turn up.

To our relief, he did. We were within a few yards of the spot where the peregrine had flown off when I heard its distinctive 'kee-kee' sound high above. 'That could be him,' I said to Peter.

Although the bird was only a tiny dot in the sky, just about impossible to see in the glare of the rapidly rising sun, Peter took out a lure – a piece of meat tied on a long line – from his falconry bag and started swinging it round, calling to the bird as he did so. The peregrine's response was electric. Within a matter of seconds the black dot in the clouds became a missile hurtling towards the earth at an incredible speed. It seemed impossible that any bird travelling so fast could slow its approach so as to avoid a neck-breaking crash, but at the last second the peregrine performed a spectacular U-turn and effortlessly grabbed the meat as he swung past. He then took the meat to the grass, where, to our delight, he hungrily tucked into his breakfast and allowed Peter to attach him to the line once more.

The South American eagle was by far the largest bird of prey that either of us had handled, however, and it was certainly the most impressive. I was intrigued to follow the harpy's progress, so a couple of days after we'd picked him up from Truro, I headed back over to see Peter and his exotic houseguest.

I'd spoken to him on the phone the day after the harpy had arrived. The X-rays confirmed the bird's wing was indeed shattered, quite high up the limb. The vet he'd taken him to had almost immediately performed an amputation, which had gone well, apparently.

I arrived to be greeted by Peter and his wife, Rose. 'How's the patient?' I asked.

'Sleeping still,' Rose said.

'That's good,' I said.

'Well, maybe not,' said Peter. 'He hasn't woken up from the operation.'

'What do you mean?'

'Well, the vet wasn't very experienced at dealing with exotic species, birds in particular, and administered what was obviously a far too heavy dose of anaesthetic,' Peter said. 'The poor thing's been comatose for more than forty-eight hours now.'

'We were worried at first,' Rose explained. 'We thought he would fall over and hurt himself again, so we sat up all night holding him in place.'

'Goodness me,' I said. 'So where is he now, then?'

'In the airing cupboard,' Peter said.

'I'm sorry?'

'In the airing cupboard,' repeated Rose. 'It was the only

place we could think of that was warm and where he fits so that he doesn't fall over.'

'This I have to see,' I said.

I followed Rose and Peter into the house and up the stairs. At the top of the landing was a pair of white doors from which was emanating a very light purring sound.

'What's that noise, the boiler?' I said.

'No, that's the eagle snoring,' Peter said.

'You're pulling my leg now.'

'No, I'm not,' Peter said, smiling. 'Take a look for yourself.' He carefully opened the door to reveal the giant brown bird standing upright on the wooden rails of the airing cupboard supported on either side by stacks of towels, sheets and assorted laundry. He looked as snug as a bug.

'I've seen it all now,' I said. 'I really have.'

It was another two days before the harpy in the airing cupboard came round fully. When he did, he didn't seem too concerned by the loss of his wing. Indeed, with Peter and Rose's help, he began eating well and soon took on the look of a healthy bird.

He had one big advantage. Big birds of prey are quite lazy creatures. As long as they have a spacious aviary and plenty of food, they really aren't too concerned about anything else. So the harpy didn't seem at all bothered by his inability to fly or get around as easily as he had done before the operation. Instead, he carried on eating and resting in Peter's aviary and made a good recovery in a couple of weeks.

Peter kept in touch with the authorities who had dispatched the eagle to him. Unsurprisingly, the European zoo that had been due to take him in decided against doing so. It took a while, but eventually someone located a zoo in San Diego that was willing to have the harpy. They had a female and were looking for a relatively tame male to make up a pair. And so it was that Peter took the eagle back to Truro Station to board a train back to London and then on to California. When the guards saw him and the giant box, they all turned rather pale, so he told me.

The harpy settled into his new life brilliantly. When Peter and Rose heard their new keepers were hoping the pair might eventually mate, they couldn't resist making a suggestion about the best way to keep any eggs incubated. Apparently the Americans didn't have a clue what they were talking about. They had no idea what an airing cupboard was.

CHAPTER FOURTEEN

A Heated Argument

It wasn't often I had the time to sit down and have a few minutes to myself, especially in the middle of a lovely summer's day. Sitting on the grassy area in the centre of the compound with a glass of Julie's lemonade, I spent a few minutes watching the assorted birds darting around the aviaries, their bright plumages almost iridescent in the sunshine. There wasn't a cloud to be seen in the powder-blue sky. For a moment at least, it felt as if all was well in the world.

Things weren't quite so relaxed in the office, a few yards away. I could hear Sue in there answering the phone almost constantly. She wasn't exactly soft-spoken, so I heard nearly all the advice she delivered too. Mostly she was giving directions to the centre or taking down an address to pass on to an inspector. I was draining the last of the lemonade from my glass when I heard her voice change in tone. 'Hold on a minute,' she said. I knew instinctively it was for me. I was getting to my feet even before she appeared at the window, shouting, 'Rex, the police want you.' I ran into the office and picked up the receiver.

'Sorry to bother you, Rex,' said the male officer at the other end of the line, 'but we've got a dog locked in a car down in the big car park at Porthtowan. There's no inspector around and we're worried it's going to overheat in there. Could you shoot over and have a look for us?'

Dogs left in cars while their owners spent time on the beach were a fairly common problem in Cornwall during the summer months. Both the RSPCA and the police had large notices up in all the county's car parks. Some, in particular those belonging to the larger visitor attractions, even provide special areas, or kennels, where dogs can safely remain while their owners are away. But it didn't seem to get the message through to everyone.

The fact is, dogs are not designed to handle heat terribly well. They cannot perspire through their skin as humans do and so rely on panting to reduce their body heat. In extreme heat, this is physically beyond them and their body temperature can rise rapidly. Confined in a hot car for twenty minutes, even with windows slightly open, a dog can easily overheat and die. I'd dealt with some unfortunate cases of this kind over the years. Owners often make the mistake of leaving their car in a shady spot, perhaps under a tree, not realising that as the sun moves across the sky the protection will disappear.

A few years back I'd dealt with a young chef who had been working late in one of the local hotels. He had returned to his rented cottage sometime in the early hours of the morning and gone to bed, leaving his two cross-bred German shepherds in his estate car, which he had parked on the grass verge outside the cottage, leaving a window slightly open.

The following morning the sun had risen quickly, turning its full glare on the car. By 9.30 a.m. the dogs had been sweltering inside. A passer-by noticed the steamed-up car and, failing to rouse the chef, who was still sleeping, phoned the police, who in turn contacted me. By the time a constable and I arrived at the car and forced open the door, it was too late for one of the dogs, and the other was in a bad way. The young lad was devastated. Exhausted by the night's work, he had overslept, oblivious of the fact his beloved dogs were in danger. Fortunately, the second dog survived and the owner doubtless learned his lesson.

When I heard from the police officer about the dog locked in the car in Porthtowan, therefore, I knew I had to come over right away. Time was of the essence. It took me around fifteen minutes to drive down to the beach. I would have got there quicker but the volume of traffic on the narrow lanes leading down to Porthtowan was unbelievable. On more than one occasion I had to reverse to let a car coming up from the beach pass by. It was almost unbearably hot in the van, even with the windows open. I feared for any dog locked inside a car in such heat.

As I finally drove down the final steep stretch of the hill towards the beach, the light reflected from hundreds of parked cars was dazzling. Beyond, I could see that the beach was crowded and the sea packed with people enjoying the surf.

Driving into the car park, I spotted a police car parked beside a red sedan and drew up alongside. A police-woman met me as I got out. She didn't look too happy.

'Sorry, Rex, I think we may be too late,' she said, shaking her head sadly. 'The dog looks to be in a pretty bad way.'

She was not mistaken. Looking into the car, I could see a small black and white collie-cross bitch lying under the steering wheel, eyes closed, tongue lolling from her mouth.

Legally, the police had every right to gain access to the car to prevent the dog coming to any harm. It took me a split second to decide on a course of action. 'Right, can you break into the car?' I said.

The male constable who was also at the scene grabbed a crowbar from the boot of the squad car. He was soon prising the driver's door open, watched by the largish crowd that had gathered.

'Can someone get a bucket or a bowl of cold water and a towel?' I said to the throng. A couple were soon running off towards the public toilets at the far end of the car park.

As the car door swung open, it was as if someone had opened an oven cooking the Sunday roast. A wave of furnace-hot air was released.

The policewoman quickly leaned inside, placing her hand on the leather front seat.

'Ouch,' she said, recoiling and looking at her hand. 'That's baking,' she said. 'Nearly took the skin off my hand.' It was hardly surprising that the whole car was like an oven. Not one window was open even a crack.

'Right, let's get her out of there,' I said.

As I lifted the prostrate form of the little dog out of the car, it seemed unlikely that anything could have survived for more than a few minutes in such an enclosed space. The signs weren't good: the dog seemed to be unconscious.

By now the couple had returned with a towel and a bucket of water. I needed to cool the dog's overheated body, so, after soaking the towel thoroughly in the bucket, I placed it on the animal, squeezing the water out so that her coat was saturated from head to tail. Soon the dog was soaked in water, but she remained almost motionless, barely breathing.

I sensed the crowd's anxiety behind me. For a few moments I feared the worst. The important thing was to keep trying to cool the dog down, so I kept soaking and squeezing the towel over the stricken creature. After about a minute, to my relief, the dog began to twitch and show signs of coming round. Soon she was breathing more steadily. Her heartbeat was very erratic and her eyes were still closed, but I could sense her strength returning steadily.

'I think she might be OK,' I said to the policewoman.

Behind me, I heard the crowd murmuring happily. There were a few 'aaaah's and even a small round of applause. I had no time for such sentimentality. I still had my job to do. For the next fifteen minutes I sat with the dog. Soon her eyes were open and she was able to drink a small amount of water. The dog's revival was a positive step, but I knew there was a long way to go. Lying in a semi-coma for so long might have caused serious damage to the dog's brain or major organs, so I knew I had to get her to a vet as soon as possible. The police said they were going to stay put and wait for the owner to return.

'We need to have a word with him or her,' the policewoman said with a knowing arch of an eyebrow. 'But thanks, Rex. Let's hope she pulls through,' she added, giving the dog a gentle ruffle.

At the vet's surgery in Truro, the nurse quickly put the dog on a drip and slipped a couple of water tablets into the bitch's mouth. I left the dog looking a lot more comfortable than she'd been an hour or so earlier.

Later that evening I received two phone calls. One was from the surgery to tell me that all was well and the dog would be ready for collection the following morning. The second was from the police, who told me the owner had eventually returned to the car, where he had been cautioned.

'We're going to prosecute him,' the officer said.

'That's for you to decide,' I said. 'Although I have to say, if it was down to me I'd throw the book at him.'

'You'd throw more than a book at him if you met him, Rex,' said the officer.

'Really?'

'Yes. A real know-it-all. He doesn't think he did

anything wrong. In fact, he was suggesting that we were outside our rights to break into his car.'

'What?' I said.

'Yes, he's a pretty aggressive character. It wouldn't surprise me if he made life very awkward for us when we get to court.'

I hung up, shaking my head in quiet disbelief. The ignorance and selfishness of some animal owners never ceased to amaze me.

I soon understood what the officer had meant about the little dog's owner. I collected the dog early the following morning and brought her back to the centre, where she settled comfortably into one of our kennels. A couple of hours later, around lunchtime, a familiar-looking car pulled into the centre. It was the red sedan we'd forced our way into the day before.

The man who emerged was a thickset character, in an expensive-looking jumper and jeans. He had a heavy Brummie accent.

'I've come to collect my dog,' he said brusquely.

'Right. Well, you'll be glad to hear she's made a full recovery,' I said, trying not to antagonise the situation.

'Of course she's made a recovery. Don't know what the bloody fuss was yesterday. The whole thing's a farce,' he said. 'The dog's used to being on her own in the car.'

I wasn't going to let him get away with this, so as calmly and reasonably as I could, I explained to him how close to death his dog had been. 'It was a close-run thing, actually. The vet said she almost suffered brain damage,'

I said. He just looked at me as if I was talking Swahili, but I persevered. 'The sun's hotter down here in Cornwall and yesterday was particularly hot. You really should have left a window open, and even then she probably shouldn't have been left in a car at that time of the day,' I said.

He was clearly in no mood to be lectured any longer. 'Nonsense. What do you know?' he said.

'Well, a fair bit. I've seen dogs die in those conditions.'

'Rubbish,' he said, clearly determined not to listen to anyone's opinion other than his own. 'Just give me the dog.'

Having signed the required paperwork, he was soon leaving, as defiant as when he'd arrived. 'Well, we'll see how much of an expert you are when you're being cross-examined in court,' he said rather threateningly.

As I watched him drive away, Julie joined me. She'd clearly been watching from the house and had overheard most of what had been said. 'Some people really shouldn't own animals, should they?' she said, squeezing my arm.

'In a word, no,' I replied.

CHAPTER FIFTEEN

You Can Take a Duck to Water

It wasn't hard to work out the identity of the two young men in the front seat of the weather-beaten Land Rover that pulled into the centre one glorious summer's evening. Its roof was laden with surfboards and kayaks, and as if that wasn't enough of a clue, the vehicle's side was emblazoned with the words 'Surf Rescue'. But as I walked out to meet the two young lifeguards, I was more than a little taken aback by what they'd brought in from the beach at nearby Crantock.

'Evening, Mr Harper. Got some little chaps that we fished out of the sea earlier this afternoon,' one said.

'Oh, all right,' I said, half expecting seabirds or one of the other forms of marine life that were occasionally brought in by the men and women who patrolled the lengthy Cornish coast. 'What are they?'

'Ducklings.'

'Ducklings?'

'Yes, ten of them. Has to be the weirdest rescue we've performed this summer.'

After weeks of fishing hapless bathers, failed windsurfers and reckless children in inflatables from the Cornish waves, the lifeguards had been called out to rescue the shelduck ducklings when they had been swept down the River Gannel. I knew that shelducks bred on the banks of the river here, using old rabbit holes to nest and lay their eggs. I also knew that, often because of human interference, young ducklings were frequently abandoned by their mothers. Shelduck ducklings are extremely photogenic, especially when they swim along behind their mother in tight formation, and can attract the attention of amateur photographers, who wade into the water to get the perfect close-up. Unfortunately, shelduck mothers don't appreciate this and sometimes take flight, leaving their offspring to fend for themselves. The inexperienced young swimmers often then get into trouble and can be carried downstream, where they become easy prey for all sorts of predators, from gulls, crows and magpies to foxes and dogs. I hadn't heard of a whole brood of ducklings being carried out to sea, however. This was a first.

The fast-flowing water had carried the ducklings down the beach, across the sands and into the surf. The little birds had been spotted tumbling around in the waves by one of the lifeguards. He'd run into the sea and started collecting the bedraggled, confused and distressed little birds. With the help of another surfer, he managed to rescue all ten ducklings and had placed them in a towel-lined cardboard box in the surf club's kitchen.

'You did well,' I told the young men. 'Especially in wrapping them up warm like that. They could easily have got hypothermia, even in this hot weather.'

As the two chaps jumped into their Land Rover and headed off, I enlisted the help of Karen and Sue. Together we placed the ten ducklings in a large indoor pen, which was already occupied by several mallard ducklings of a similar age. They were soon enjoying the warmth of the infrared lamp that was suspended over the pen. Duck-lings are not difficult to feed and the brood began tucking into a meal of chick crumbs in a shallow container of water.

We'd had more than our share of ducks, chickens and geese at the centre over the years – both wild and domestic. Sometimes the domestic birds that arrived with us were just unwanted, or their owners could no longer keep them due to sickness or old age. Others were picked up as strays after being dumped by their owners. In one memorable instance a group of unwanted chickens were found on the island in the middle of a busy roundabout.

The one that always stuck in my memory, however, was a white gander who was brought in from a home in Plymouth. The gander had been kept by a man who lived alone and had developed a passion for collecting all manner of birds. Unfortunately, he wasn't the brightest of characters and had kept them all in a single room in his house. When the RSPCA were called in by worried neighbours, they found more than fifty birds, ranging from tiny zebra finches and pigeons to various poultry, living in cramped cages in the same room. The man had allowed conditions to deteriorate terribly and there were thick layers of dried droppings and feathers all over the room. Among the birds rescued was a six-month-old white gander that had apparently been in the man's menagerie since it was a young gosling. It was the only goose among the collection of birds.

The gander's development had been seriously impaired by living in such terrible conditions. Starved of sunlight and a decent diet, his beak and legs were a very pale pink, rather than the normal healthy orange, and his plumage was lacklustre and scraggy due to a lack of washing. The gander, along with many of the other birds, was brought to us, but his behaviour was strange from the beginning.

When we placed him on the grass in our large-bird compound, the gander was horrified and ran under a shed to hide. It wasn't hard to understand this peculiar behaviour. The gander hadn't interacted properly with humans or birds in his old home. He must have been overwhelmed by hearing noises he couldn't respond to and being able to roam free. He also made extremely odd guttural noises that didn't sound anything like a normal goose. These were no surprise either. In the cramped, deprived environment he had grown up in, there was probably no reason to have learned to speak goose.

For the first few days we kept the gander isolated from

the other birds in a cage that allowed him to watch but not interact directly with them. This seemed to settle him and after a week or so he began pecking grass and even discovered the pond. Unfortunately, this too was alien to him and he had no idea what to do in the water. He sat on the edge of the pond, dipping his head in and going through all the motions that a goose would go through while having a bath. The only difference was he did it on dry land. But then one day he fell into the water by accident. The gander immediately sank like a stone and had to be saved from drowning by an alert member of the centre staff who had heard the plop as the bird fell in the water.

Inspecting the gander afterwards, we weren't surprised at his lack of seaworthiness. His feathers didn't have any of the normal waterproofing you'd expect to find on a goose, because the oil gland near the base of his tail was blocked. As a result, he couldn't spread waterproofing oil on to his plumage when he preened himself.

That evening we dried the gander with a hair-dryer, unblocked his oil gland and left him contentedly preening himself under an infrared lamp in an indoor pen. It was as if his life had been transformed. From then on he was a different bird.

Over the next few weeks the gander started swimming on the pond, eating grass and sitting out in the sun with the rest of the compound's birdlife. The sunshine brought the colour back to his legs and beak too. He was soon looking a picture of health, his plumage a gleaming white.

At that time we had no other waterfowl in the compound, but one day a small white female call duck was brought in as a stray. The two white birds soon struck up a firm friendship, spending all their days together. Despite their very different statures, the mismatched pair became inseparable. When the breeding season arrived not long afterwards, it was no wonder that their natural urges began to take hold. This, however, proved as frustrating for them as it was amusing for me and the rest of the staff. Once or twice a day the tiny duck would squat down and wait for her huge partner to mate with her. The gander would do his best to satisfy her, gently taking hold of the duck's neck at the back of her head and trying to mount her. For a moment or two the duck would be completely hidden beneath a mountain of white feathers, only to suddenly reappear behind the gander, having walked out from between his legs. It was hilarious to behold.

The gander's recovery was soon complete, but I knew he was unlikely to find a new home elsewhere. So, after consulting with Julie, I turned him into the fields to join our own small flock of birds.

Shortly afterwards the RSPCA centre took delivery of a new consignment of eight geese, which had been found on a farm, again in terrible conditions. Among them was a young female goose. Once rehabilitated, we decided to put her with the white gander.

At first he was bemused at the sight of a bird that looked exactly like him. He had never seen one before. But they soon paired up and began mating. It took two attempts to get it right. The pair's first eight eggs were infertile, which didn't surprise me at all given the gander's unhealthy life, but later they produced eight healthy goslings, which they doted over as mother and father.

Every now and again the transformation we were able to make in an animal's life would touch me unexpectedly. It didn't happen often, and nor could it, given the number of animals passing through, but for some reason it happened with the white gander. I could never explain it, but when I watched him fretting and fussing over his goslings each day, I'd think back to the condition he'd been in when he'd arrived with us. He'd seemed like a freak, a totally abnormal bird, but given the chance, he'd proven himself to be very normal indeed. I was glad to have helped him.

The shelduck ducklings were nowhere near as challenging as the white gander. In the days and weeks that followed their arrival they did well, and together with their mallard companions were soon enjoying the comparative freedom of the outdoor waterfowl enclosure, rapidly exchanging their baby down for juvenile plumage.

As ever, I was careful to keep the birds as wild as possible. If they were going to survive back in the wild, they had to have no meaningful human contact, so the birds were left completely alone except for when their food was provided in troughs twice a day.

The young shelducks and mallards matured well. It

wasn't long before their wing feathers had developed and the fully grown birds were flapping their wings vigorously as if to say, 'OK, I'm ready.' It was time to release them.

Releasing captive reared young birds is always a worry. No matter how careful you are in selecting a release site, the fact that the birds have none of the normal guidance from their parents means they are particularly poor at finding their own food sources and are also vulnerable to predator attack. I knew I had to be careful in releasing the young ducks into the wild. Fortunately, I knew the right location to take them. One morning I placed all the young shelducks in a pair of carrying boxes, loaded them into the back of the van and drove them to the RSPB reserve at the Hayle estuary, a half-hour or so away.

With its extensive mudflats, this was an ideal place to let the shelducks re-enter the wild. I arrived to find the tide out and the flats alive with life of all kind, from swans and Canada geese to a variety of ducks. I could even see several young shelducks feeding in the distance. Perfect, I thought to myself.

Donning a pair of long wellingtons, I tucked a box of ducks under each arm and set off across the mud. It wasn't easy picking my way through the sticky flats with two boxes, but I eventually arrived at the river's edge, opposite the shelducks, which were now feeding on the mud no more than ten or twenty yards away.

I opened the carrying boxes and watched as the young ducks took a long look at the river before taking to the water and dabbling around in the shallows. They seemed content, and one or two seemed to have spotted their fellow shelducks on the mud nearby.

Convinced all was well, I collected the boxes and set off back across the mud towards the distant van. Again it was heavy going and halfway back I stopped for a breather. Glancing back the way I had come, I couldn't quite believe what I saw. There, arranged in an almost perfect straight line behind me, were the ten shelducks. They were tracking me. For a moment I laughed to myself. I felt a bit like the Pied Piper. But my amusement quickly turned to alarm. How had this happened?

The golden rule when working with birds is to avoid imprinting them with any kind of connection to humans. Something had gone wrong here. I didn't know whether these young ducks regarded me as a father figure, a source of safety or simply someone they found fascinating. Whatever it was, they had reacted to this strange and threatening new environment by latching on to something with which they were familiar: me. This is potentially disastrous, I told myself. What should I do?

There was really only one option. Dumping the boxes on the mud, I retraced my steps through the mudflats to the river, making sure the young ducks followed me. Sure enough, they turned tail and waddled along behind me, once more in a disciplined single file, like soldier ants on the march.

My best chance of shaking them was to somehow integrate them with the other shelducks, so I headed back to the spot where I'd seen the wild youngsters feeding a few minutes earlier. To my relief, I found them still wading and swimming in the shallows on the opposite side of the mudflats. I'd clearly not brought the two groups close enough together the first time. I'd led the ducks to water but I'd not made them drink. I wasn't going to make that mistake again, so this time I picked my way even further across so as to bring my young shelducks as close to the wild ones as possible. I then held my breath. 'Come on, you lot, make some new friends,' I muttered.

For a few moments the ducks circled round me, but it wasn't long before one or two spotted the fun their wild mates were having and were swimming off in their direction. Soon all ten had joined them and I was forgotten, thank goodness. Within a few minutes the two groups had integrated as if they were lifelong friends. Things looked promising but I knew I couldn't head off in a hurry again. If I wanted to avoid distressing them and having them track me, I would have to wait until the young ducks were settled and felt secure.

I sat down on the upturned hull of a sunken boat and waited for a while, taking in the scene. It was hardly a chore; there was so much to see – and hear. The air was filled with bird calls, from the bubbling trills of curlews to the piping of oystercatchers. Then I heard the most evocative sound of all, the musical strumming wings of mute swans as a pair flew low overhead on their way to the river. Not far away, some redshanks waded in the shallows. They were the watchdogs of the estuary, always on the lookout for predators and ready to raise the alarm. Elsewhere, small flocks of dunlin scurried along the muddy banks of the river, and in a flash of brilliant blue a kingfisher sped along inches above the water. I could have sat there for hours taking in these wonders of nature. Unfortunately, I had to get back to work. After a quarter of an hour I decided it was time to leave. All seemed well with the ducks, so I slowly moved away, glancing back every now and then to ensure that I wasn't being followed. To my relief, I wasn't; indeed, the last time I looked round I saw the ducks waddling off in the opposite direction.

As a final precaution, when I got back to the van I fished out my binoculars and scanned the mudflats and the distant river but there was no sign of the shelducks at all now. Mission accomplished, I told myself. But only just.

CHAPTER SIXTEEN

A Ghost in the Attic

The attic was hot, dusty and shrouded in darkness, despite the blazing sunshine that was trying to break through the cracks in the old slate roof above me. As I forced myself further through the small trapdoor and shone my torch along the eaves, there was no immediate clue as to who – or what – was living up there. Was it a cat or a mouse, or was the attic really inhabited by a restless spirit? Only time would tell.

I'd been called in to investigate the attic by Janet, a lady from Truro who had a long association of helping the RSPCA. She'd been asked to visit an old antique shop, part of a parade of commercial properties on one of the oldest terraced streets in the centre of Truro. The owner, along with many others on the street, had heard strange scuttling and scratching noises emanating from the attic that ran along the top of the adjoining buildings. The odd, sometimes rather violent noises had unsettled both customers and staff, leading one or two to suggest it was a ghost. An elderly customer had added fuel to the fire by revealing that there had once been a particularly gruesome murder in one of the houses. Perhaps it was the tortured soul of the victim, a young woman who had been strangled by her violent husband, she unhelpfully suggested. Apparently, one of the younger shopgirls had turned white and almost fainted on hearing the tale.

The shopkeeper who had called Janet had a more worldly theory. She was convinced it was an animal, perhaps a mouse but, given the scratching, more probably a feral cat. She had rung Janet, a specialist in homing strays in the city, to investigate. Unfortunately, Janet was now in her seventies and less nimble than she had once been. From the descriptions she'd been given by the shopkeeper, she'd been persuaded it might well be a cat. Truro's feral cat population were masters at making themselves at home in the city's most inaccessible spaces. The space available up in the attic would have made it an ideal hideaway. But when Janet had been faced with the climb into the cramped and claustrophobic space, she'd blanched at the prospect and called me.

Janet had told me what she'd found so far. She'd also laughed that some believed the attic to be haunted. I'd had one or two close encounters with strange phenomena over the years, including what may well have been a ghost at Ferndale when we'd first moved in, so I'd come along armed with a torch, a cat trap and an extremely open mind.

*

It was far from the first time an RSPCA official had become an amateur ghostbuster. Cornwall has always been rich in ghost stories. Even the county's coat of arms carries an image of a spirit – the red-billed chough, the bird that, according to legend, was inhabited by the ghost of King Arthur. Since my earliest days working with the RSPCA, I had regularly come across stories of supposedly haunted buildings. The most memorable involved a tall chimney on the edge of Perranporth that had begun emitting strange noises at night.

The tall brick chimneystack was a remnant of Cornwall's tin-mining past and had stood there largely ignored for more than a century, but then a few years back people began talking about a scraping, hissing and even an eerie snoring sound that came out of the chimney at night. Naturally, all sorts of rumours were soon spreading about the cause of the curious noises. The more practically minded locals suggested it was air rushing up from the underground mineshafts that lay deep beneath the chimney. More fanciful souls suggested it was the ghost of a victim of a mining disaster from the previous century. The sinister noises were the sounds of the miner trying to scratch his way out, then hissing with despair before falling asleep and snoring, exhausted.

Several people had tried investigating the noise but had been defeated by the chimney's architecture. There was no ground-level entrance to the stack, and although the top was open to the sky, it was about eighty feet high so it was impossible to climb up without specialist equipment. Even if someone had been able to climb it, the building looked distinctly wobbly, with loose bricks at the top. The fact that no one could breach the chimney walls only added grist to the rumour mill, of course.

It took the intervention of Ralph, then the local RSPCA chief inspector, to finally shine a light on the mystery. Ralph was a keen amateur historian and took a great interest in anything relating to old Cornwall. Armed with nothing more sophisticated than a thermos of coffee and a pasty, he set himself up in some bushes next to the chimney one spring evening and began a night-time vigil. For the first few hours all was quiet.

It was as he sat quietly sipping his cup of coffee that a silvery moon appeared through the clouds, lighting up the old stone chimney fully for the first time that night. Almost immediately Ralph noticed a movement in the sky. He watched in silence as a ghostly shape silently winged its way to the top of the stack, landing expertly on the crumbling bricks.

In an instant the night air was filled with odd noises. Muffled hissings, strange snapping sounds and scufflings started coming from deep inside the chimney. For a few moments the ghost vanished, only to reappear on the chimney's rim as the noises stopped as suddenly as they had started. Ralph watched on as the ghost spread its wings and took to the air, emitting a blood-curdling screech as it flew overhead.

Well, that's solved that little puzzle, Ralph thought, smiling to himself, doubly delighted to have solved the mystery and discovered that a family of barn owls were being raised inside the old chimney.

The sounds that passers-by had been hearing at night were the owl chicks calling excitedly as one or other of the parent birds arrived on top of the chimney with a mouse or vole. The wheezy snoring was one of the barn owl's natural calls. The ghost of Perranporth had been laid to rest.

As I travelled to investigate the strange noises in the attic in Truro, I remembered Ralph and the chimney with a quiet smile. I was fairly certain I was going to find a similarly mundane explanation to the strange goings-on there.

It was a baking-hot morning and conditions in the attic were not pleasant. Squeezing myself up through the trapdoor and into the dusty space under the tiles, I ran the beam of my torch along the floor and into every nook and cranny, but there was no trace of a cat – or indeed any other creature. As I crouched on my knees and looked further into the attic, the only discovery was a series of labyrinthine joists and beams that must have dated back a couple of hundred years. They made moving around the long, spacious attic extremely difficult.

Having explored the area around the doorway, I bent myself over double and squeezed through the V-shape of two crossing beams into another section. This time I did find something: the remains of two pigeons. This, to me, made a cat even more of a likelihood. The two birds had been ripped to pieces by a skilled predator and very little remained of either pigeon. Feral cats are merciless and efficient killing machines. These two may well have been its meal at some point in the past few weeks.

In an ideal world I would have explored every corner of the attic, but after half an hour or so rooting around in the shadows I came to the conclusion that the space was simply too tight and it was impossible to do so. Besides, after squeezing my way through half the attic, I was covered in a combination of dust, cobwebs and large spiders. I was ready to head home. I hauled up a cat trap and placed some tinned cat food on the platform inside it. If there was an animal up here, it would almost certainly be tempted.

My instincts proved correct. Around nine o'clock the following morning I got a phone call from the shopkeeper. 'There's a cat in the trap. Or at least I think it's a cat,' she said. 'It's making a heck of a racket. Doesn't sound like it's very happy.'

'I'm sure it's not,' I replied. 'Don't go near it. Just leave it there and I'll be over as fast as I can.'

Within the hour I was re-entering the dusty attic to be greeted by the sight – and sound – of an extremely angry feral cat. She was small in stature but a fully grown lion couldn't have displayed more aggression. Her ears were laid flat back on her head and her green eyes were blazing in the dingy light. She was snarling and growling and pawing at the cage. I had no doubt that if she'd been able to get at me, she would have tried to scratch my eyes out.

Shining the torch on her to have a closer look, I saw why she was so animated. She was heavily pregnant and clearly feared for her unborn kittens more than herself.

'All right, old lady, let's get you sorted, shall we,' I said, easing myself up through the gap and covering the trap with a blanket.

Beneath the blanket I could feel the cat trying to slash away at the material. When I carried the trap through the antique shop a few minutes later, the cat was still protesting wildly. The shopkeeper looked horrified.

'We've got a wild one here,' I said. 'But don't worry – I know just the place for her.' We were soon safely installed in the van and heading back to Ferndale.

It was always hard to find homes for feral cats. Older cats, like this one, often reacted badly to being caged and would never settle. It was pointless even thinking about them as domestic pets. They would be dangerous, apart from anything else. Occasionally farmers would be willing to take them in to control rodents, but most farms are inundated with cats of their own. I didn't hold out much hope.

I couldn't put such a feral cat in with any of the centre's feline patients. She would have to remain in isolation. Fortunately, I'd already worked out that I had the perfect place for her back at the farm. We had recently finished haymaking and the loft over our small milking barn was full of bales. Golden brown and smelling of summer, they were piled up to the roof in the loft over the milking area. This would make a perfect place for the feral cat and her soon-to-be-born brood. In the short term, it would provide her with an undisturbed area where she could have her kittens in peace and safety. What her long-term future would be I had no idea at all.

Arriving back at the farm, I put those worries to one side and carried the cat into the barn, shutting the door behind me. When I let the cat out of the trap, I wasn't at all surprised when she immediately shot out and raced towards the mass of bales stacked up in the loft. She was soon squeezing herself between them and disappearing from view. I had a feeling I wouldn't see her again until she'd safely delivered her litter. I left her – and nature – to it.

In the days since her arrival at the farm, the feral cat, or Lady, as I'd come to call her, had kept herself scarce, but there was no doubt she had remained in the safety of the hayloft. Each evening I'd taken in plates of food and saucers of milk, and early each morning I'd return to discover she'd consumed every scrap.

I guessed she must be close to giving birth, and one morning, four weeks or so later, I got final confirmation. I'd finished my rounds at the centre and was collecting the empty food plate when I heard a distinctive squeaking sound coming from the loft. I looked up to see three tiny kittens tottering on the hay bales. When I climbed the ladder to have a look, I discovered they were extremely healthy-looking individuals. I picked up the little balls of fluff and held them in my hand. At first they hissed and fizzed away, but they soon quietened down when they realised that humans weren't so bad after all.

Their mother remained hidden throughout, however. She was not yet so trustful of humans. Nevertheless, I felt rather pleased that we'd been able to help her deliver her kittens in peace. My next objective was to make sure she didn't produce any more.

I gave her another few weeks to wean and finish preparing the kittens for the big, wide world. After those weeks were up, I began removing the kittens, each of whom found homes with ease. When the last of them had been removed, I put my plan into action. As I left Lady's food out one evening, I slipped a small amount of tranquilliser into her meal. An hour or so later I slid back into the barn to find her sleeping soundly. The following morning, back in a cage once more, I took her to the vet's surgery, where she was spayed.

Given Lady's wild nature, the vet used disposable thread for the sutures so there was no need for her to be handled again. It was now up to her how she led the rest of her life. I was not going to be able to place her in a home, so a couple of days later I left the door of the hay barn open so that Lady could reclaim her freedom, if she wanted of course.

Our hope was that she would live on the farm with us. She seemed to want the same thing. Lady became a ghostly figure on the farm. Every now and again we would see a streak of dark tortoiseshell fur flashing around the buildings. At other times we would catch a glimpse of the little cat sitting on the windowsill of the barn watching the cows file in for the morning milking.

She was clearly at home now, although she remained unwilling to get too close to us humans. When Julie or I spoke to her, she ran off immediately. She would then remain out of sight for a day or two before reappearing again, often at a particular spot on the windowsill where Julie and I would leave a saucer of milk.

As time passed by, Lady became trusting enough to sit beside Julie as she milked, yet she would never allow herself to be touched. That, we now accepted, was a bridge too far. We didn't mind. We'd come to accept Lady as a part of the furniture at the farm, which made the tragedy that befell her all the harder to bear.

We had been experiencing a real problem with an invasion of rabbits and had set snares several fields away from the farmyard to help deal with the numbers. I really didn't like using traps of any kind, but in this case I felt we had no option. One morning I was checking the lower fields for rabbits that might have been caught overnight when I discovered Lady dead in one of them. She had been choked by the wire noose. I had no idea she was roaming so far from the farm. I had assumed that because she was eating everything I gave her she would have no need to extend her hunting range at night-time.

What made her accidental death even harder to bear was the fact that cats will often sit quietly in a snare waiting to be released. As a boy, I'd accompanied many a rabbit trapper on his morning rounds and had set many a cat free from a trap so that it could run home unscathed. But Lady was no tame domestic cat, she was a thing of the wild, and she had fought to escape. It had been her undoing.

I was absolutely devastated by the discovery. Lady's progress at the farm had been a real source of pleasure to me. I'd become rather attached to her. That morning a kind of fury descended over me. Driven by my grief at losing Lady, I went around the fields collecting every snare that I'd laid. I then marched up to the farmhouse and burned them all in the Aga. I haven't set another snare since and nor will I.

CHAPTER SEVENTEEN

Slippery Customers

The summer holidays were drawing to a close and the first hint of autumn colour had appeared in the trees. Down in the valley, the raucous sound of the rooks gathering each evening had become noticeably louder. The seasons were changing.

I was in the yard one morning when Jim, the postman, arrived with an official-looking letter in a manila envelope. The back of the envelope was marked with an official stamp and read, 'Magistrates Court, Truro'. Inside was a summons, requiring me to appear in court as a witness in the case of the man who had locked his dog in his car at Porthtowan. In the weeks that had followed the incident, I had put it to the back of my mind. The letter brought the memory of that hot summer's day flooding back.

'Wonder whether that chap is still determined to blame everyone but himself,' I said to Julie, filing the letter away in the kitchen.

'Wouldn't be surprised. Didn't seem like the sort to accept he'd done something wrong,' she commented.

'No,' I said, drifting off into my own thoughts for a moment.

Since rescuing the dog, all sorts of ideas had gone through my mind. I'd begun to wonder, for instance, whether the court would see things in their true light. Perhaps a jury would decide that I had acted too hastily. Perhaps they would have sympathy for the owner's argument that the dog was used to the heat. Who knew, perhaps ultimately I might be the one in the dock. If it was proven I had acted inappropriately, the RSPCA would almost certainly have to discipline me. And what would happen then? Might I be removed from my job as warden of the centre? Who was to say?

I pulled myself up before I let this train of thought go too far. 'Funny how you can begin to feel guilty about something even when you know you're in the right,' I said to Julie.

'How can you possibly have been in the wrong? Don't worry about it.'

Unfortunately, that was easier said than done.

I arrived at Truro Magistrates Court a few days later to be briefed by our solicitor. At the other end of the corridor, outside the courtroom, I saw the familiar face of the dog's owner. The man had been given the option of pleading guilty by post but, to no one's surprise, had driven down from Birmingham to enter a plea of not guilty. What was slightly surprising, however, was the fact that he had not hired a solicitor and, our own solicitor informed me, was intent on defending himself. In a smart suit and with his notes in front of him, he looked quite an impressive character. He looked even more so when the case got under way. When the clerk read out the charges, he stood in the dock shaking his head slowly, as if he couldn't believe the audacity of what he was hearing.

When he was asked how he pleaded, he puffed himself up, stuck out his chin and looked directly at the magistrate. 'Not guilty,' he said defiantly.

The case began with the police outlining what had happened on that sweltering afternoon. Both the constables I'd met in the car park gave evidence. After each had been guided through their evidence by the prosecution lawyer, the man cross-examined them. There were more than a few exchanged glances on the prosecution side as he did so.

'Are you aware of the maximum temperature a canine can withstand without distress?' he asked the female constable.

'No,' she said.

'Oh, I see. So you didn't know a dog can happily survive in eighty or ninety degrees of heat?'

'No.'

'And did you know that there are wide variations in the temperatures that different breeds can withstand?' he went on.

'Well, no, but the dog was clearly in distress. If we didn't act . . .'

'A yes or no was all I required. No further questions, thank you, madam.'

When the RSPCA's vet took the stand, the man was even more aggressive in his questioning. The vet told the court that, in his estimation, the dog would have died if she had been left in the car for half an hour that day.

'How did you calculate the dog could have survived for half an hour?' the man asked the vet.

'Experience. I've seen many cases of dogs dying from overheating in cars here in Cornwall,' he said.

'But every dog is different, is it not?'

'Yes.'

'Did you know that my dog is used to being in a car for long periods?'

'No, but—'

'No further questions.'

He seemed worryingly professional. Was he a vet, or a lawyer? Or both?

When it came to my turn to give evidence, I took the oath and recounted as accurately as I could remember what had happened that day. During my cross-examination, the man again behaved as if it was me and not him who was facing charges.

'How long after you arrived in the car park did you break into my car?' he asked.

'No more than two minutes,' I said.

'Was that long enough for you to weigh up the situation properly?'

'Yes, it was,' I said emphatically. 'The dog was semi-conscious. She would have been dead in minutes.'

'How do you know that?'

'Because I've seen it happen before.'

'But how do you know it was going to happen here?' he persisted.

'Because, as I say, I've spent my life looking after animals and there was no other possibility. She wouldn't have survived. Plain and simple as that.'

As I climbed down from the witness box, I felt a little deflated. I'd stood up to the man, I felt, but I still wondered how all this had gone down with the magistrate. I recognised the lady who was sitting behind the bench. She was a well-known and highly respected local magistrate with long experience. Our solicitor assured me the magistrate had encountered cases like this before and had come down hard on negligent owners. As the case drew to a close, however, I wasn't sure she'd encountered a defendant as resourceful as this.

Fortunately, the man himself had to give evidence next, and when our solicitor began questioning him, the sheen of confidence began to slip.

'Why did you leave the dog for so long?' the solicitor asked.

'I lost track of time,' he said. 'I had been going back to see the dog every half an hour or so.'

'But when we got there, the car park attendant said the dog had been on her own in the car for at least two hours.'

'Well, he must have been distracted when I went back.'

'That's unlikely. He said he had been specifically waiting to see you to tell you your dog was suffering. You say that your dog is used to being left in the car on her own.'

'Yes.'

'Do you never take her for a walk, then?'

'Yes, of course, but there are times when I have to leave her.'

'Would it not be easier to leave the dog at home?'

'It's my dog and I can take her where I want,' he said, the sudden snappishness in his voice drawing a raised eyebrow from the magistrate.

'Regardless of whether the places you take her are suitable. Like a beach car park on a hot summer's day. No further questions.'

After we'd all given evidence, we filed outside to the lobby, where we waited nervously for the verdict. At the other end of the corridor, the man paced around in an agitated state. He wasn't quite as confident as he had seemed in court.

After what seemed like an age the clerk reappeared and summoned us back into the courtroom. I took a deep breath.

The man was asked to stand and the magistrate quickly announced her decision. 'On the charge of cruelty to animals you are found guilty,' she said.

'Thank goodness for that,' I said, turning to our solicitor.

The magistrate then went on to fine him £100 plus additional expenses. Moments later we all filed out of the courtroom. The man left the court scowling, but chose not to make eye contact with me or the police officers.

The officers, the vet and I shook hands with each other briefly, all relieved, I think, that justice had been served.

'I thought he was going to get away with it,' I told the solicitor.

'So did I – for a minute. I just needed to keep him talking. I knew he'd slip up.' He smiled. 'You know what they say – give them enough rope.'

My day in court had left me feeling a little claustrophobic. I wasn't used to being cooped up indoors sitting around doing nothing for such a long period of time, especially not when the weather was as glorious as it was today. I was relieved to get back to the centre later that afternoon.

Karen and Sue were winding down for the day and there were no inspectors around. Things were pretty quiet, in fact. Ominously so. That, of course, meant I could almost certainly expect something unusual to crop up. It did, and, even more predictably, just as I was thinking about heading back to the house for a spot of supper.

When I answered the phone, the lady on the other end of the line was quite beside herself with worry. 'I don't know what to do. I've got a snake in my kitchen, a big 'un,' she said.

'Whereabouts are you?' I asked, wondering whether she was near an inspector who might be on call.

'Porthtowan.'

'Oh, all right. Not far from here, then,' I said. I could hear barking in the background. 'Have you got a dog in the house with you?' I asked her.

'Yes, he's in the kitchen, trying to scare the bloomin' thing away.'

'Well, tell him not to do that,' I said. 'If he carries on like that, he'll get a nasty bite.'

This only made her more agitated. I could hear her shouting, 'Jesse, Jesse, come away. What do I do? What do I do?' she said, verging on the hysterical by now.

'Right, I need you to do three things for me,' I said.

'Yes.'

'The first is to try to remain calm.'

'OK.'

'It's very, very rare that snakes bite humans. They only do it when they are provoked or attacked, so if you leave it alone, it won't hurt you.'

'OK.'

'The second is to give me your address over there in Porthtowan.'

'Right,' she said, before giving me the name of a street I knew was on the hill overlooking the sea.

'And what's the third thing?'

'If you can get back into the kitchen and put the kettle on, I'd like a tea with milk and no sugar. I'll be there as fast as I can.'

The prospect of dealing with snakes was not something that bothered me in the slightest. Quite the opposite in fact. I'd been something of a fan of snakes since I was a young boy. I could remember vividly my first encounter with one. I'd been sitting on the edge of a quarry, looking for a kestrel's nest, when suddenly this huge snake appeared below me weaving its way up the slope. It was a typical grass snake, with a bright yellow collar and greenish-brown body. It was, however, unusually large. In fact it was huge. It must have been between four and five feet in length, with a thickset body. In the years since, I've never seen such a specimen.

Snakes don't have very good hearing and rely more on vibrations around them, so as I was sitting perfectly still, this one didn't notice me for some time. When eventually it did, the reaction was immediate. Turning with lightning speed, it sped back down the side of the quarry towards a small lake at the bottom, surrounded by beds of reeds, into which it vanished. Since then I'd been rather fascinated by snakes. Indeed, I felt they were badly misunderstood and mistreated creatures.

It wasn't often I was called out to deal with them. The last time had been when I'd travelled to the village of Mylor, set in a creek on the river Fal, where someone had reported a grass snake with its head caught in some netting in their garden. I'd arrived to discover a large crowd gathered around the snake. It had got itself hopelessly stuck in the fine netting, which was being used to cover a strawberry patch.

Grass snakes, although not venomous, can look and sound pretty impressive, especially when they open their mouth wide and hiss loudly. The crowd were standing at a safe distance as this one hissed at them. Fortunately, it was an easy enough job to free it. Having borrowed the lady of the house's nail scissors and tweezers, I cut around the area where the snake had got trapped, allowing it to wriggle free. To applause from the watching crowd, the grass snake immediately lunged out of the netting and arrowed its way across the lawn to the shelter of a thick hedge, never to be seen again.

While I was firmly of the view that people generally overreacted to the presence of snakes, I never made light of the threat they could present, especially exotic ones. The most frightening case I had come across was that of a python that a family in St Austell adopted as their household pet. Zoe, as they knew her, had been acquired when she was young and had been a small snake early in her life. She'd been allowed the freedom of the house and had happily grown up around the family's several children. Each of them was quite comfortable having Zoe slithering around their shoulders as they sat on the sofa watching television. Pythons, however, do grow to quite extraordinary sizes, and Zoe was no exception. By the time she reached maturity she was over twelve feet in length, with a body that was in places as thick as a small tree trunk.

I was called in by the concerned parents to give them some advice. Zoe had always been, and remained, a gentle creature, but they could see the snake was changing physically. Their worry was that she would alter temperamentally too. Apart from anything else, the snake had become too big for the house. The family were having to step over the python as it slept on the floor, and visitors were becoming very nervous of coming into the house. It didn't take long to reach a conclusion. In their hearts I think they knew what to do but they wanted someone else to say it. My advice was for them to find Zoe a new home and, if the children wanted, replace her with a smaller snake.

The parents agreed and I arranged for Zoe to be accepted at Newquay Zoo, where there were already several pythons in residence. The family were sad to see her go, but it didn't take long for us all to know the decision was the right one. Zoe became a different animal at the zoo. She became aggressive and her keepers had to treat her with extreme caution during her first months there.

There was little doubt in my mind that this transformation could have occurred in her former home, and goodness knows what the consequences might have been. A large, powerful snake like that could quite easily have killed, or even swallowed, a small child. It didn't bear thinking about what might have happened if we hadn't acted.

Three-quarters of an hour or so after speaking to the lady, I was driving down the steep hill that leads into the picturesque coastal village of Porthtowan. I couldn't help marvelling at the scene. Out at sea, the golden sun was dipping below the horizon, its light suffusing the whole Cornish coast with a radiant red glow. It reminded me, once more, how privileged I was to be living and working in such a beautiful part of the world.

The village was busy with holidaymakers, some just leaving the beach, others out for an early evening stroll before supper. As was so often the case at this time of the year, negotiating the small, tightly packed streets in the van wasn't easy.

Eventually arriving at the address I'd been given, I was shown into the kitchen, where I discovered the lady's elderly collie still barking. The object of his anxiety was coiled up in a corner. It took me an instant to recognise what it was: an adder. It was a beautiful snake with a quite pale body that made the dark zigzag lines along its back stand out in sharp relief before forming into the telltale V-shape on the top of the adder's head.

In my opinion adders undeservedly get a pretty bad press. They are by nature shy creatures and will, wherever possible, do all they can to keep well out of the way of people. They cannot always make their escape, however, and when cornered, they are capable of delivering a nasty bite, which was my concern here. Dogs, as it happened, are particularly vulnerable and can die as a result of an adder bite. I'd seen many a dog brought in to us with a telltale swelling around the head, having been bitten by an adder while nosing around in the undergrowth. I always sent them straight to the vet.

The adder in the kitchen was clearly as anxious as the other occupants of the house. Its head was resting on its coils and was facing the dog in a threatening manner. I knew this wasn't a good situation, so my first job was to get the collie out.

'Jesse, Jesse,' I said, distracting the dog, then grabbing his collar. He wasn't terribly pleased about it, but I managed to lead him out of the kitchen, entrusting him to his owner. 'If you could keep him out of harm's way for five minutes, I'll be able to sort this out,' I told her, before easing my way back into the kitchen and shutting the door behind me.

Taking a moment to weigh up the situation, it wasn't hard to see how the snake had got into the house. A set of steps led up to the back door, which was wide open. The snake had clearly slid down the steps but then found itself trapped, unable to travel back up them again. With the dog gone, the adder wasted no time in trying to climb the steps. Snakes can normally climb very well, but these steps were made of smooth stone and were very steep. Realising it wasn't up to the task of scaling them, the snake retreated and coiled itself up defensively once more, this time at the base of the steps. It lay there, its eyes watching me as if warning me not to come too close.

I knew that, if I moved in too near, the adder would try to bite me. I needed something to manipulate the snake from a distance. In the hallway I'd noticed a collection of walking sticks in a rack and so popped out to grab them. The lady had shut herself in the living room with the dog and I could hear her talking quietly to him. At least they were out of the way now, I told myself.

When I gently touched the snake with one of the sticks, it hissed but didn't strike. Instead, it once again tried to negotiate the steps. I needed to help it, so, moving in a little closer, I managed to get a walking stick under each end of its body. Being careful not to move too sharply or suddenly, I then helped ease the snake up each of the steps until it was out of the back door. When it reached the garden path, it slithered away at speed. The adder was soon disappearing into the back of the garden.

'I think it's learned its lesson. It won't come in again,' I said, leaning into the living room where the lady and her dog were sitting in front of the television.

'I do hope not,' she said. 'And thanks so much for coming over here at such short notice. Sorry I didn't get to make you that cup of tea. I couldn't bring myself to step into the kitchen. Would you like one now?'

'No, thanks,' I said. 'My supper will be getting cold. I'd better get back to Perranporth.'

Driving home in the gathering twilight, I felt tired. It had been a long, eventful and unusual day, even for me. In both cases, however, things had gone my way. It wouldn't always do so, of course, but for now I savoured the sweet smell of the day's small successes.

CHAPTER EIGHTEEN

Tiger and Mervin

Walking through the centre of Truro one morning, I heard the familiar strains of a piece of violin music drifting through the autumnal air. I knew immediately where it was coming from: the old cobbled square near the entrance to the cathedral. I also knew who was producing the rather tuneful melody.

As usual, I found the scruffy figure of Mervin sitting on the pavement, legs crossed, playing his fiddle while shoppers and tourists dropped coins into his battered old hat. Mervin must have been in his early fifties, though it was hard to tell. He had a mass of long, salt-and-pepper hair and a thick, extremely shaggy beard that obscured almost all of his face. So far as I knew, he had no real home and slept in shop doorways or in the city's parks every night. He'd been a fixture on Truro's streets for years now, appearing during the summer and autumn months before heading off to other, unknown pastures during the winter and spring.

As usual, lying beside Mervin's violin case on a blanket on the pavement was a dog, a small beagle-cross-terrier bitch he called Tiger. Tiger was a lovely mix of black, white and tan. She was a quiet and well-trained dog, and seemed completely content with her lot. I'd got to know the pair of them over the years, at first through taking an interest in Tiger. Aware that his life wasn't exactly comfortable, I would often ask Mervin how the dog was doing. His reply was always the same: 'What, that bloody useless thing? You can take it if you want.' He usually accompanied this sentiment with a half-hearted kick in the direction of the dog. I took Mervin's words with an extremely large pinch of salt. You only had to spend a minute in their company to see the pair were devoted to each other. I'd seen them walking around the city a couple of times and Tiger would always trot along beside Mervin, tight at heel without a lead. The way she always looked up adoringly at her master, with her tail wagging like a metronome, suggested to me that they were utterly inseparable.

Once, purely for some fun, I had taken Mervin up on his offer to remove Tiger from his care. 'OK, Mervin, if you really don't want her, I'll stick her in the van and find her a new home,' I had said, half smiling. 'I can think of quite a few families who'd fancy a little dog like Tiger.'

Mervin's response was exactly what I expected. He wiped his nose with the sleeve of his filthy old coat, cleared his throat and shook his head. 'No, I know you RSPCA buggers. If you take the dog, you'll put her to sleep faster than you can say, "Jack Robinson",' he growled. 'So you can get lost.'

'Only kidding, Mervin,' I had laughed. 'Any fool can see that the pair of you are like a married couple.'

'Hmmph,' he'd said.

Beneath his gruff, aggressive exterior, I knew Mervin cared deeply for his dog. He had barely a penny to his name most of the time, yet I knew that if times got really tough, he would always make sure Tiger was well fed and cared for by someone.

Mervin was just finishing playing his piece as I approached him today. As usual, I bent down to give Tiger a gentle pat and dropped a couple of coins in the hat.

'Ah, the RSPCA fella,' Mervin said, putting his violin and bow to one side on the blanket. 'I need to have a word with you about my Tiger.'

'Oh, yes,' I said, giving the dog another stroke on the head, noticing at the same time that she looked larger than when I'd last seen her.

'What it is, see, is this bloody useless dog has gone and got herself in the family way. She's having pups any minute now,' he said, scowling through his beard, 'and there's no way I can keep a flaming pack of bleeding puppies, is there?'

'No, I suppose not,' I said. 'So what would you like me to do, Mervin?'

'You'd better take her and put her down or whatever it is you do over there at the RSPCA,' he said, staring at the pavement, unwilling to look me in the eye.

I was rather taken aback by this. 'All right, Mervin,' I said, trying to buy myself some time to think. 'I've got a few errands to run but I'll be back in a while. Let me see what I can do. I'm sure we can do something to help.'

'Better be quick, then,' he said, running his fingers through the straggly expanse of his beard, 'or I'll chuck the bleeding useless thing in the river.'

I had a couple of calls to make in the city centre and so left Mervin to his music for half an hour or so. By the time I returned to him, I'd come up with what I thought was a sensible plan of action.

'OK, Mervin,' I said, 'I've had a good think about this and the best thing would be if I take Tiger back to the RSPCA centre with me so that she can have her pups there.' Mervin just nodded, again staring at the pavement, as if he was terrified I might see some emotion in his face. 'It will be more comfortable for her there.'

'And then what?' he grunted.

'Well, I reckon she should stay with us for six or seven weeks after her litter arrives, so that she can rear and wean them properly.'

'Hmmph.'

'Then we can find good homes for all the puppies, and when that's done, I can bring her back to you so that the pair of you can carry on as normal together. How does that sound?'

Stony-faced, Mervin leaned over to his violin case and pulled out his instrument. As he put the fiddle to his chin and tightened his bow ready to start playing once more, he looked at me, almost dismissively. 'Do what you want with her,' he said with a shrug of his shoulders. 'Don't know as I want the bleeding thing back, though.'

I didn't bother replying.

A couple of minutes later I reversed the van down the narrow street and lifted the heavily pregnant Tiger into a dog cage in the back. Judging by the size of her, she was going to give birth within days – if not hours.

Mervin pretended to be absorbed in his fiddling, but as I was about to shut the rear doors, he stopped playing abruptly and got up. He picked up the old blanket from the pavement, shuffled over to the van, opened the dog cage and placed the blanket carefully round the little dog, giving her a little smoothing rub. He then turned and went back to his violin. He didn't say goodbye to his dog of course. That would have been too public a display of affection. But he didn't need to. I knew what he was really feeling.

Moments later, as I got into the van, Mervin was fiddling away furiously. There was no doubt in my mind he was playing louder, faster and with much more emotion than normal. I suspected his music was revealing his true feelings.

Tiger was a delightful little dog. She settled into life in the centre's kennels easily. Four days or so after arriving she went into labour and produced four extremely healthy mongrel puppies. She took to parenthood immediately and was a devoted mother. During the first couple of weeks, when the puppies stayed pretty much glued to her, she licked and cleaned them, let them suckle on her teats whenever they wanted and let them sleep on her tummy in an unruly heap when they were full. When someone she didn't know approached her, she would growl intimidatingly as if to say, 'Don't you dare come near.' I felt pretty sure she'd learned the growl from Mervin.

During this time there was no real indication that she was missing her eccentric master. She didn't have time to dwell on him. But as the puppies grew and the centre staff began weaning them off her milk and on to solids, she began to show signs of pining for her grumpy old soulmate. By the time she'd been with us for a month or so she began taking an interest when people visited the centre. Her ears would prick up when she heard unfamiliar voices or footsteps approaching the kennels. I felt sure she was listening for the familiar gravelly tones of Mervin.

I'd kept him informed of Tiger's progress throughout the first weeks she'd been with us. I'd see him most weeks, almost always in the same spot, fiddling away. He would feign disinterest of course, grunting monosyllabic replies or even ignoring me completely. Every now and again I'd wonder whether he really was glad to be rid of Tiger. I never believed it for very long.

We had no trouble at all placing Tiger's puppies in decent homes. Within seven weeks of the litter's arrival the first of the pack was leaving us for a home in St Austell. With homes already allocated for the rest, Tiger's time with us was drawing to a close, so when I headed off to Truro that week, Mervin's pitch near the cathedral gates was my first port of call.

To my surprise, however, there was no sign of him. I didn't worry about it too much, but when I visited Truro again a couple of days later and he was still nowhere to be seen, I started to feel a little concerned. I asked around the local shops to see if anyone had heard anything. A newsagent who Mervin used to visit for his cigarette papers told me that he'd heard the violinist had moved on. 'Someone said he's gone to Plymouth,' he said.

Well, that's great, I thought to myself. How on earth am I going to get Tiger back to him in Plymouth?

Back at the centre, I called an inspector I knew who was based in Plymouth. I told him the story of Tiger and asked him to keep an eye out for Mervin, providing him with a detailed description.

'Shouldn't be too hard to find him, Rex,' he said. 'Can't be that many bearded violinists living rough in Plymouth.'

'I hope not,' I said. 'But if you find him, tell him to give me a ring here at the centre.'

It was only a day or so before the phone went in the office and I heard a familiar rasping voice at the other end of the line. 'I suppose you expect me to spend my money on a bleeding railway ticket to come down to pick up that damn dog,' he said.

'Well, it's up to you, Mervin,' I said, 'but Tiger's missing you, I think.'

'Hmmph.'

'When do you think you'll be able to make it down here?'

'I'll be at Truro Station at ten o'clock tomorrow morning.'

'All right.'

'But don't be late or I'll be off. I ain't waiting around all day.' And with that the phone went dead.

In the kennel later on I saw Tiger eagerly looking around at the latest batch of visitors to come to see what was left of her litter of puppies.

'Don't worry, old girl,' I said. 'You'll see him tomorrow. And he won't have changed a bit.'

The following morning, just past nine thirty, after giving Tiger a generous breakfast, I loaded her into the dog cage and set off in the van for Truro Station. A heavy mist was hanging over the higher ground that lay between us and the city, making driving slow and difficult. We pulled up at the station just as the Plymouth train was arriving, a couple of minutes earlier than scheduled.

Tiger and I waited in the van, watching the crowds of people emerging and heading down the hill into Truro city centre. It had got rather steamy in the vehicle, so I had opened the window next to me. I'd also let Tiger out of the cage so that she could stick her head out. As each new face appeared, Tiger would stick out her head and prick up her ears excitedly, only to withdraw back into the van again when it turned out to be a stranger.

The train had been pretty full and what must have been a couple of dozen people had emerged before a familiar figure loomed into view in the morning mist. Mervin looked slightly better turned out than normal and was wearing a big, dark military-style coat with shining buttons. He had his violin case over one shoulder and a giant brown army rucksack over the other. These were clearly all his possessions. The rucksack had a tin cup and a pair of ancient muddy boots dangling from the side.

The moment Tiger saw him she stuck her head out of the window and started yelping, barking and wagging her tail excitedly. The moment I opened the van door she was away, her beagle ears flapping wildly as she ran along the pavement.

Arriving at her master's feet, she jumped up to greet him, pawing at his coat. Mervin had seen me, so made barely a gesture of recognition towards the dog. 'Another bloody mouth to feed,' he muttered in a rather shaky voice as he approached the van.

'For you, Mervin, yes, but for me it's one less to cater for.'

'Hmmph,' he grunted, rubbing his beard.

'Now, Mervin, I've got something important I want you to do,' I said.

'What's that, then?'

'I want you to take this to the vet whose address is written on the back.' I handed him an envelope that had the name and address of a vet in Truro on the outside and a voucher entitling him to a free spaying operation for Tiger inside.

'What's this?'

'Something that will make sure Tiger doesn't produce any more unwanted pups.'

'We'll see,' he said.

'No, make sure you do it in two or three months' time, when she's ready,' I said. 'It won't cost you a penny, and Tiger will thank you for it.'

'Hmmph.'

I knew he would go. He wouldn't let Tiger leave his side again in a hurry.

'Right, I've got to be off,' Mervin said, hauling the rucksack back into position on his shoulder. 'If I'm going to feed this wretched hound, I'd better earn some money.'

'OK, good luck,' I said. I gave Tiger a farewell pat and climbed back into the van. I sat there for a moment watching Mervin as he wandered down the hill in the direction of the cathedral spire, which rose above the rooftops. His faithful companion was at his heel, her tail wagging away constantly. They were about to turn the corner and disappear from view when I saw him stop and bend down. It was clearly a routine they'd been through a million times before. When Tiger jumped up and placed her front paws on her master's thighs, Mervin began patting and stroking her and rubbing his nose against her wet snout. When I saw him looking back up the hill towards the van, I ducked out of sight. I wouldn't have wanted him to see the lump in my throat.

CHAPTER NINETEEN

Ravens in the Tower

I was writing up a report on the previous day's events when the phone went. The caller was a rather well-spoken gentleman who introduced himself as the Warden of the Spires at Truro Cathedral. He had my attention immediately. Ever since I first visited Cornwall as a boy, in the 1940s, I had been in awe of Truro's crowning architectural glory, the nineteenth-century Anglican cathedral that dominates the city skyline from almost every angle. Arriving on the train for the first time after the war, the magnificent building, with its soaring trio of spires, was the first thing that struck me. It was, I think, one of the spectacles that made me feel so drawn to Cornwall and its many beauties.

The warden explained that there was a problem with the cathedral's population of ravens. 'We've started finding young ravens stranded on the cathedral lawns. One or two have been found dead. We can't quite work out what's happening,' he said. 'Today we came across a pair of them. They aren't quite ready to fly, so they can't get back up to their nests in the tower. Would you be able to come and have a look?' he said.

I was surprised by the call. Ravens had been nesting high in the spires of the cathedral since as far back as anyone could remember. To my knowledge – or indeed that of the colleagues I talked to later that morning – there hadn't been any problems with the birds in living memory. Intrigued, I headed over to Truro at lunchtime.

I pulled up in the car park alongside the monumental building and spent a moment taking in its majestic beauty once more. Its three spires are what catch the eye most immediately, but there is much more to the cathedral than that. Its lower levels, for instance, are built of light yellow Bath stone and are a maze of pillared galleries and carved ledges.

The interior of the cathedral is every bit as imposing as its exterior, and as I stood in the aisle waiting to meet the Warden of the Spires, my eyes drifted upwards to the vaulted ceiling, stirring memories of the many magical choral concerts Julie and I had attended here over the years.

I was still lost in thought when the warden, a distinguished-looking man in his sixties, arrived to bring me back down to earth. 'Mr Harper, isn't it? Thanks for coming over at such short notice.'

'Have you had any problems like this before?' I asked, after shaking hands with the warden.

He was keen to answer my questions. 'No,' he said.

'That's the peculiar thing. The ravens have always lived up on the roof and have always got on with their lives without bothering anyone. There are some peregrines up there as well, but they seem to get on OK.'

'Yes, they would,' I said.

Ravens and peregrines have an uneasy relationship, but tend to put up with each other. I'm not sure quite why this is. Perhaps the raven's superior brain helps it to avoid attacks by its aerobatic neighbour, or perhaps the raven's massive beak makes the peregrine a little wary.

'So we are all at a bit of a loss as to how the birds have been falling off the roof like this,' he said.

I shared his bemusement. As we walked out of the cathedral and round the gardens, it struck me that the spires weren't unlike the raven's natural habitat, the high cliffs of the north Cornwall coast. There, young ravens fly around the crags near their nest until their wings are strong enough to allow them to venture further afield. It was the same on the cathedral roof. In the past I had watched the youngsters flying between the lofty spires and building up their strength, so there seemed to be no reason why suddenly things should go wrong. The only explanation I could think of was that maybe they had lost their parents and had left their nest too early when starvation had forced them to go searching for food, but ravens were pretty hardy birds and that seemed unlikely, unless there was a disease of some kind killing the older generation. If there had been, of course, it would have manifested itself in the young birds, which it hadn't. So all in all it was really quite a mystery.

The warden took me to the back of the cathedral and showed me the two ravens he had discovered that morning. The pair of young birds were cowering against the wall. Picking them up and examining them, they appeared unharmed and in good condition. Both were carrying enough weight, so weren't going to starve, but equally they weren't fully fledged and were certainly not going to be able to fly back to the roof hundreds of feet above.

Stepping back from the building, I looked up to the buttresses and turrets far above and soon spotted the adult ravens perched near their nest site in one of the towers. That ruled out one possibility: they had not deserted their young or been killed. The mystery deepened. For now, however, my priority was to try and reunite the youngsters with their parents.

'There's a staircase, if you'd like to try that,' the warden said.

'I'd rather not,' I said. I was familiar with the tight corkscrew staircase that wound its way up to the upper reaches of the cathedral. Years earlier a friend had been studying the peregrines at the top of the tower and had offered to take me up with him. I quickly declined as I have no head for heights of that kind. Cliffs I could manage, but not high buildings. 'Is there another high spot?' I asked.

He directed me to the new restaurant that had been constructed adjacent to the cathedral. Borrowing a ladder from a nearby shop, I placed it against the restaurant wall and climbed up, carrying the two ravens with me. I then placed them on the guttering above. Immediately the two birds scrambled and fluttered up to the apex of the roof, where they sat calling to their parents, high above.

Climbing back down from the roof, I watched developments from the cathedral lawns. I expected to find the adults had moved down towards their young, but looking up, I could see they hadn't. After a while the youngsters decided to try moving up the roof themselves and flew up twenty or thirty feet of the cathedral wall. They were making good progress when, out of nowhere, the air became thick with a very different – and unexpected – sound. Gulls.

From some other corner of the tower, six herring gulls suddenly appeared and headed straight for the two struggling ravens. Within a split second they were pecking at the younger birds and buffeting them with their wings. The impact on the ravens was immediate. The gulls hit one of the unfortunate birds out of the air with such force that it crashed to earth, landing on a tombstone and breaking its neck. Even from thirty or so yards away I could see it was dead. At least the other one was more fortunate. It too fell to earth but it landed on the grass, where I saw it tumbling to a halt. The mystery was solved.

I knew that large numbers of herring gulls had begun to abandon their nesting sites on the north Cornish cliffs for the more comfortable surroundings and easy pickings around the centre of Truro. Many had made their homes on the flat roofs of buildings in the city centre, including some close to the cathedral. Now it seemed they had spread their wings and established themselves on the cathedral itself.

This was bound to be bad news for the ravens. Gulls detest ravens, with good cause. The big black birds can rob eggs from unattended nests or even take young gull chicks, so it wasn't surprising that the newly arrived settlers had launched a quick offensive against the cathedral ravens, targeting the young ones as they took their first wobbly flights between the ledges on the towers. This explained the discovery of the fallen ravens immediately.

Any ideas that I might have entertained of getting the remaining young raven back up to its parents were now forgotten. There was no point. Even if the youngster was reinstated on the lofty heights, it would not be long before the gulls discovered it and sent it crashing to earth once more, possibly for the last time.

There was, however, one more avenue of approach. I had noticed some tall sycamores on the edge of the cathedral lawns. If I placed the raven in one of the loftiest trees, it might just be high enough to allow the adult ravens to fly down and feed the youngster.

Dragging the ladder round to the most accessible of the trees, I placed the young raven on as high a branch as I could manage and let it go. Encouragingly, it began taking short flights from branch to branch, moving upwards all the time until it had reached the very top of the tree, at least sixty feet up.

From the ground, I could see it perched there singing out to its parents, who were calling back from their position high in the tower. The flight now was much more manageable for the little bird: fifty feet or so across, but only twenty or so upwards. It was even easier for the parents to fly down to their offspring to relieve its anxiety and perhaps help it to safety.

Come on, I said to myself. One of you make a move.

But it was not to be. In spite of, or perhaps because of, their intelligence, wild ravens are distrustful of humans, and although I had made sure to hide myself in a position where I was not too visible, the adults simply refused to come down to feed their chick. Instead, after a few minutes spent calling to it, they both took off, circling the main tower before wheeling away towards the river and their feeding grounds. The sense of frustration I felt was immense. My plan had failed, and to make matters worse, I was now left with the problem of the young raven, which was still calling hungrily from the treetop.

Again I surveyed the options, but this time there were none. There was no way that I could climb the tree to recapture the bird. As the early afternoon traffic began to build, I reluctantly decided to give up and headed back to the centre. I felt uneasy and worried about the little raven for the rest of the day. It wasn't long before the two of us were reunited, however.

Early the following morning the centre got a phone call reporting a raven walking around the main street in Truro. According to the rather concerned caller, it was picking its way along the road amid the bustling morning traffic and had narrowly missed being run over on several occasions.

Armed this time with a large catching net, I drove to the area around the cathedral, where I quickly located the raven. I was pretty sure it was the same one that I'd lifted into the trees the previous day. After another day and night left to its own devices, it looked ruffled and was calling loudly every now and then for food. It was clearly getting desperate.

Trying to wield the long-handled net to trap the raven among the thickening morning crowds was not easy, however. More than one passer-by gave me a very peculiar look indeed. Some clearly thought that I was intent on catching the bird to put it down. One forced me to explain what I was doing, which lost me more precious time. As I tried to track the raven along the busy pavement, the press of the pedestrians made my job almost impossible. The first time I got close to the bird and swung the net it collided with someone's shoulder and clattered to the ground, sending the raven fleeing. Luckily for me, its strength was by now sapped to such an extent it only managed a short journey to the ledge above a shop, where it sat calling mournfully for its parents once more.

The ledge was tantalisingly out of reach, even with the extended net. All I could do was wait until the raven decided to fly back down on to the street. Fortunately, my luck was about to change. Moments later the raven set off across the street fluttering its wings sluggishly, before flying straight into the plate-glass window of Lloyds

Bank. Stunned by the impact, it slid down the clear pane and into a thickly planted windowbox, from which I managed to extract it and place it in a carrying box. It was soon safely installed in the aviary back at the centre, where it guzzled down its first meal in days.

We'd had many ravens at the centre over the years, but two ravens in particular taught us more than most. The most remarkable bird we'd ever taken in at Ferndale was, of course, Odin. He'd been with us for more than fifteen years now. Odin had come to us after being taken illegally from his nest by some young boys. The boys had hand-reared and kept him as a pet in their home. As a result, Odin had become completely humanised and had no fear of people. In fact he loved their company and sought it out at all times. We had tried to relaunch him back into the wild many times, but always without success. We'd sworn never to allow the same thing to happen and had applied the lessons we learned with Odin to every raven that came our way and they were usually able to return to the wild.

Things hadn't gone quite so well with a young raven called Thor, however. He had arrived suffering from minor injuries and spent only a few weeks with us. In keeping with our policy, he was kept isolated from the public and not befriended in any way by our staff so that when we came to set him free he would have every chance of surviving. When that day came, I took him to the bottom of our fields. I let him go and he flew off in the direction of the coast. As I watched him disappear into the distance, I felt pretty confident he'd prosper in the wild. How wrong could I have been? Instead, Thor was drawn to people and set himself up with a home on the cliffs at St Agnes, where he perched above the summer crowds that thronged the beaches.

At first he would watch as people headed home in the evening and gorge himself on their left-over sandwiches, fish and chips, and ice cream, but Thor was a smart bird and it wasn't long before he progressed to stealing the odd sandwich from under the noses of picnicking parties and scaring children as he stalked around the deckchairs. Thor spent his nights away from the beach in a large garage in St Agnes, where a rather eccentric lady kept an immaculate vintage Rolls Royce. It was a choice that was to prove his undoing.

Thor decided to sleep on a beam that was directly above the gleaming vehicle. The consequences were inevitable. Each morning the lady would discover her pride and joy streaked with Thor's liquid droppings. When the irate owner rang the centre to complain about what was happening, I was called out to visit the property after dark one evening. It was the devil's work catching Thor. At one point I had to climb on top of the precious Rolls Royce's bonnet and was petrified of leaving a dent. But I eventually captured the mischievous raven. Thor spent the rest of his life at a nearby bird garden.

So as I drove the cathedral raven back to the centre, I knew I mustn't repeat any of these mistakes. I decided that the centre, with its steady stream of people coming and going, was not the right place for the bird. Besides, we lacked a seclusion aviary to isolate the raven.

Fortunately, I knew of the perfect place for this chap: Paradise Park, a well-established and much respected bird garden at Hayle, a half-hour's drive away. I had known the owners from the start of their enterprise and had assisted them with bird problems in the early days, so they were more than willing to help me out. David, the park's curator, agreed to keep the raven for a few weeks, then release it on the north Cornish coast. It was a relief to know the bird would soon be back in a natural environment.

Given the situation at the cathedral, however, I didn't expect it to be the last time I'd be called out to deal with its threatened population of ravens, and so it proved when the ravens bred again the following year. The cathedral called twice, both times to deal with chicks that had fallen to earth. I dealt with them in the same way, moving them on from the centre to Paradise Park and, eventually, freedom in the wild.

To no one's great surprise, it wasn't long before the ravens had stopped breeding in the cathedral tower. Instead the gulls went from strength to strength, establishing more than twenty nests on nearby roofs. They caused many problems, all brought about by our own untidy habits, but who could blame them when every rubbish dump and littered street provided them with an easy meal? They forced the authorities to erect scaffolding to scrub the once-golden stone clear of the accumulated mess they – and man – had inflicted on one of the wonders of our corner of the world.

CHAPTER TWENTY

Amber

It wasn't much after 5 p.m. but the nights were closing in fast and so the lights were already on in the office. In the gloom outside I heard the sound of something rattling down the lane towards the centre. I looked out to see an RSPCA horsebox looming into view and bumping to a halt by the main gate. Karen, Julie and I were expecting its arrival and, once it had safely reversed into the yard, headed straight to the back of the vehicle, where we began unbolting the doors and lowering the ramp.

As we'd been warned, the young female pony lying in a thick bed of straw at the back of the horsebox was in a very bad way indeed. Little more than eight months old, she was soaked, bedraggled and absolutely exhausted. I guessed she was suffering from hypothermia, which was hardly surprising given where and when she had been discovered: on the roadside up on Bodmin Moor, exposed to the wild October elements. If it hadn't been for the keen eyes of passing motorists, she would almost certainly have died there. The couple had been driving in across the windswept moor from Devon late that afternoon when they had slowed to allow a long trailer loaded with potatoes to cross the road. As they sat waiting, they noticed what looked like an old brown rug lying in a roadside ditch. When the lady saw the rug moving, alarm bells rang. The husband and wife pulled over and walked back in the gathering dusk to discover the brown object was a pony, clearly in distress, lying on its side in the ditch. They concluded that it must have been knocked over by a passing lorry or van.

Not everyone who encounters situations such as this is blessed with the common sense to deal with it. Fortunately, this couple were and they jumped in the car, headed for the next phonebox and called the RSPCA via the emergency services. Within thirty minutes of their call a team of three inspectors had arrived at the scene. The pony was so weak it had required little effort on their part to half lift, half drag it into the deep straw of the horsebox. They had then headed straight for Perranporth and the welfare centre.

As I moved in alongside the pony, it was clear that she was in a parlous state. Her breathing was weak and she was obviously suffering from exposure to the intense cold and wind on Bodmin Moor, one of the most open and wild spots in the entire south-west of England. The good news was that she hadn't suffered any serious physical injury. There were no broken bones or cuts. She had probably fallen over into the ditch after being dealt a glancing blow or suffering a near-miss from a passing vehicle, perhaps knocking her head in the process. There were major concerns, though, not least her weak condition, which – without the right care – could easily deteriorate.

With the help of the three inspectors, Julie and I moved the pony from the horsebox to the barn, where we bedded her down in the thick layer of fresh straw we'd laid out in advance. We then gathered around the pony and gently used some old towels to dry off her long, wet coat. It was little wonder the horse was so cold: she was absolutely saturated. The barn was well insulated and warm, but we put in an electric heater to raise the temperature a few degrees for the long night that lay ahead.

We knew that the pony's chances of survival would depend on the next twelve hours or so. If she managed to sleep through the night, then she might well make a good recovery. But this was by no means certain and she could easily slip away, so Julie and I spent the night taking it in turns to check on the pony every couple of hours. Neither of us got much sleep.

As we lay awake for most of the night, Julie and I couldn't help reminiscing about some of the other horses we'd taken in over the years. They'd provided us with more than their share of laughter and tears.

The case most similar to this was a horse called Bracken. He was now grazing happily in the fields at the rear of the centre, something that would have seemed impossible when he first arrived with us after being abused by the farmer who owned him.

Perhaps the most memorable horse to have passed through our hands, however, was Lightning. We'd been living in our previous home, the Rosery, when we'd been offered him by a friend, a local chemist who had bought him from a rather disreputable breeder. Our friend had bought the pony for his three children, but, as is so often the case, they had tired of the hard work that goes with caring for a pony. We hadn't really any room for him but our children had been so keen on having a pony we had ignored the practicalities and simply said yes. As luck would have it, a kindly neighbour offered to let us graze him in a nearby field, so when he arrived he settled in quickly.

Lightning was a little Dartmoor pony, a dark bay gelding, twelve hands high and about four years old. Ponies are great characters, strong-willed, naughty and without the good manners of horses. Lightning displayed all these characteristics, and more. Even so, Lightning was always a popular member of the household, particularly when one of the children had a birthday party. Visiting friends would queue to be given rides on the pony as he was led up and down the lane. Our children absolutely adored him, and he seemed fond of them too. He allowed them to groom him, tack him up and ride him around the field and lanes. Lightning was very much in charge, however. If he decided to stop to eat an especially attractive morsel in the hedge, or climb halfway up a wall to see what was in the next field, he would do so, regardless of what his young riders had in mind. Lightning was on the short side and I always felt rather silly sitting astride him, with my feet almost touching the ground either side of his stout little body. I felt like something out of one of those Thelwell cartoons. Lightning was used to children riding him, so at first he was distinctly unhappy at being told what to do by a more experienced rider. I say 'experienced', but I was not such a great horseman that I could prevent Lightning putting me over his head several times, always when I least expected it!

Lightning would have stayed with us for years more, I'm sure, if he hadn't developed a condition known as sweet itch, brought on each year in the late spring as the result of being bitten by midges. The insect bites were concentrated around his mane and tail, causing an allergic reaction and terrible irritation, which made him rub and scratch constantly. He even bit the affected areas, which only aggravated the condition. Vets told us to rub sulphur ointment into the sores and cover the vulnerable areas with bandages, but our efforts were to no avail. Our lack of space was, in the end, our undoing – we were without a stable or shed to put Lightning in in the evening, when the midges were active. So, with heavy hearts, we gave him to some friends who had plenty of shelter.

Julie and the children all shed a tear the day Lightning was led off in a horsebox. Deep down, I think they'd all been trying to fill the gap he'd left ever since.

Daylight broke soon after 7 a.m. Julie had done the last check at around 5 a.m., so while she enjoyed an extra half an hour in bed, I headed out into the soupy morning light to check on the pony. The wind and rain of the previous days had lifted and the sun was peeking from the east.

There was mixed news when I opened the barn door. On the one hand, the pony had eaten none of the hay or nuts that we'd left out for her. On the other, she was standing, albeit shakily. Feeling her withers, I could tell that she had regained a lot of heat and was breathing much more freely. She was out of the woods, it seemed.

With the sun up, it was reasonably warm for the time of the year, so I opened the barn door and let the new arrival wobble her way into the grassy field at the back of the farm. Perhaps she would eat something more natural, I reasoned.

Watching her pick her way across the field, it was obvious the pony was still very weak. As she dropped her nose to sniff at the grass, her hind legs seemed distinctly uneasy, shaking like those of a boxer about to collapse to the canvas. She looked half-heartedly at the grass, debating whether it was worth eating. With winter drawing in, it was past its best but there were odd patches that looked more succulent than others, to our eyes at least, and it was to these that I tried to steer her. Even this failed to tempt her. She seemed too weak and depressed to get down to grazing properly.

I was soon joined by Julie, who said she'd been unable to get back to sleep. She tried the same routine. Horses were something of a speciality with Julie, and to no one's surprise, the pony came to her a lot more readily than she had to me. Julie gave her a soothing rub of the neck and held a piece of grass to her mouth, but she broke away, finding it not even remotely appetising.

'This is going to be a long haul,' Julie said with a slow shake of her head. 'I've got a feeling this little girl's been treated rather badly by whoever it was who kept her up on Bodmin.'

'Well, remember the state poor old Bracken was in,' I said, gesturing to the healthy-looking horse munching away at its breakfast near the gate to the compound.

'True,' she said, nodding. 'And that time Lightning ate so much fresh grass he got colic.'

'That's right,' I said. 'They usually come round.'

'It just makes my blood boil that people neglect horses like this,' Julie said through gritted teeth. 'If I ever got hold . . .' She didn't need to finish the sentence.

As we got on with our morning chores, we left the pony picking her way unsteadily around the field. We'd asked Mike, our local vet, to come over and would decide on our course of action after he'd examined her.

Mike arrived midway through the morning. Leading the pony back into the barn once more, he confirmed that she had no external injuries, but he administered a couple of injections, one of an antibiotic and the other to help restore her appetite. His greatest concern, however, was her general condition.

She was growing her thick winter coat but it was still possible to see her backbone and ribs through the hair. There were also patches of bare skin where the hair had been rubbed or scratched away. As Mike gave these patches a closer look, it didn't take long to discover the cause. The pony was infested with huge numbers of lice. Her back, neck and upper legs were all thickly infested with the parasites. Even Mike had seldom seen so many lice on one pony. He recommended a good dusting of louse powder for the next few days at least.

Julie stayed with the little pony for most of the rest of the day, tempting her with hay, pony nuts, carrots and anything else that might get her eating. When I returned from some calls that evening, I could see that things were improving. The pony had a much brighter look about her.

'She's eating. Well done,' I said.

'She's doing all right,' she said, 'but she's not eaten enough to get her stomach working.'

'That's no good, is it?'

'No, it isn't,' Julie said, rubbing the horse. 'Is it, Amber?'

'Amber?'

'Yes, that's what I've decided to call her.'

'Fair enough,' I said. 'She's your horse.'

'Yes, she is,' she said, giving me a look with which I was all too familiar. I had a funny feeling the gap that Lightning had left all those years ago might have been filled at last. Amber wouldn't be leaving us in a hurry.

CHAPTER TWENTY-ONE

New Arrivals

The night was cold and damp, and in the lower fields of the farm, a light mist was clinging to the ground. Huddling together for warmth in the lee of a hedge, at least Julie and I could be grateful that the rains of the past few days had eased.

With a pair of our Jersey cows due to calve, we were checking them every few hours. Julie, who was the expert when it came to looking after livestock, was a strong believer in natural outdoor birth being healthier for both cow and calf, so over the years we'd spent many a magical night under the stars watching over the cattle. Despite the dampness and the chill in the air, we felt a sense of anticipation once more tonight.

This year we'd had a pair of cows artificially inseminated. With their gestation period now drawing to a close, Julie had been watching for the telltale signs of labour and late this evening she'd seen one of the expectant mothers leave the herd and wander off to stand by herself under a copse of trees. Years of experience told her that birth wouldn't be too far away.

We'd never quite understood why, but most of our calves seemed to be born at night. Perhaps it was the privacy this time of the day afforded them, or perhaps it was simply the law of probability. At this time of the year, November, it was dark for more than twelve hours. Whatever the reason, it seemed the darkness was encouraging nature to take its course once more. From our position near the copse, we could see from a distance that the cow was walking round in tight circles, sniffing skittishly at the grass as she went.

'Not long now,' Julie whispered. 'She'll lie down in a minute, I bet.' Julie had acquired a sixth sense about calving and it proved accurate once more that night.

A few moments later the cow was lying down as her contractions became more intense. Often this stage could last for some time, with the cow getting up, circling round some more, then lying back down again and again until she sensed the calf was ready to emerge. But in this case things seemed to be moving along at a pace. The almost full moon was now a fitful presence behind the slow-moving clouds, but when it did appear, it lit the fields up with a dim glow. As it broke through briefly, we were able to see the cow lying down, straining, and two sets of pale hooves just visible.

We knew these were the crucial moments when our help might be needed. If all went well, with a couple more heaves from the cow the calf would slip naturally out on to the grass and we would be redundant; but if there was any sign that the mother was having difficulty, for instance if the calf was breeched or was in a bad position for delivery, then we would need to intervene.

We had done so on many occasions over the years. Mother Nature could be capricious and cruel at times. Some heifers were not cut out to be mothers and every now and then one would reject or even try to kill her first calf. When this happened, obviously we had to intervene quickly, removing the calf and bottle-rearing it.

The other common problem we faced was premature births. Once, a cow began displaying signs of going into labour weeks before she was officially due. The premature calf was born twisted and deformed, with legs of different length. The poor creature was so grotesque and misshapen that we had no choice but to call in the vet to administer a lethal injection. Julie was devastated by the loss, which she blamed on the vast amounts of crop spray that had been used in fields locally around the time the calf was conceived. The spray, delivered from overhead by a plane, had been so toxic that when it drifted across our fields, three hives of bees had been wiped out. Of course we could never prove it, and when Julie confronted the company that had done the spraying, they dismissed her with a patronising 'Don't worry, missus, it will do more good than harm.'

Tonight, however, nature smoothly took its course. Within minutes a glistening calf slid out and was snuffling and shaking its ears to remove the membrane from its nose and head. The miracle of birth never ceased to invoke a sense of wonder in Julie and me. Once more we watched as the cow raised herself to her feet and made vocal contact with the new arrival with a series of low, guttural sounds, then positioned herself over the calf so that she could begin the job of licking it clean with her rough tongue. Her thoroughness was admirable. Every inch of the calf's body was carefully cleaned before she stood back to admire her work and encourage her newborn to take the next step into the world.

The calf began moving its legs in an effort to stand but, completely incapable of coordinating its limbs, found them collapsing beneath it. Undaunted, it tried again – and again and again – until it was finally standing up, sniffing the air, searching for its mother's udder and the first taste of her colostrum. This stage was often a matter of trial and error on the part of the calf. Some calves would wobble their way to the teat immediately, while others would search around their mother's anatomy, sucking on everything but the teat before discovering the source of their milk. This was one part of the process that really did have to be left to nature. There was no point in showing the calf what to do – it had to work it out for itself. This one, however, was quick on the uptake and was soon gulping down its first meal.

'I think we can leave them to it, don't you?' Julie whispered, as mother and child huddled together under a hedge, the heat from their bodies rising into the cold night sky.

'Think so,' I said. 'Unless you want to stay here to watch the sun come up?'

In years gone by we'd stayed in the fields until the first bright streaks of dawn had begun lightening up the eastern sky and the first birds had begun twittering. With another calf due any day or night, however, we both knew we should grab some sleep.

'Perhaps next time,' Julie said, and we headed up the hill towards the lights of the house.

Breeding and rearing animals had become an intrinsic part of our life since we'd moved to Ferndale. Over the years we'd watched all sorts of creatures produce their young, from sheep and goats, chickens and cows to cats and dogs. They, in turn, had produced moments of wonder, sadness and not a little laughter.

Our small herd of Jersey calves had provided their share of funny moments. Early on, when she'd first started breeding cattle, Julie insisted on having the bull calves castrated during the first weeks of their life. She'd heard of bulls developing sexually at a young age and their rampant testosterone levels causing problems among herds on other farms and so had decided to act accordingly.

The policy had worked well enough, but then one day she got talking to a farmer friend. Julie always sold the calves at eight or nine months of age. The farmer suggested she could save herself time and money by leaving the bull calves intact. 'Calf don't need it if he's leaving that young,' he said authoritatively.

How wrong he was. That year Julie left intact the three or four bull calves that arrived. By the time one of them was six months of age, he had developed a nature that was amorous to say the least. When Julie went into the field to feed the cattle, the young bull would snort and toss his head in an aggressive manner that was far more mature than his age.

There were several heifer calves in our small herd and the young bull was soon taking an interest in them and trying to jump on them, despite being repelled by a series of violent kicks from the females. One afternoon Julie was feeding the calves when the bull tried it on with a very young heifer, who was standing next to her at the feeder. Julie shooed the bull away but instead of taking no for an answer, the randy youngster tried to jump on Julie instead. Luckily she managed to escape being knocked to the ground.

The final straw came one morning soon after this incident when Julie had fed the calves and was walking towards the gate at the top of the field. She suddenly sensed that something was behind her, and without turning round ran as fast as she could and hurriedly climbed over. Her intuition saved her skin. Just as she cleared the gate the young bull charged straight into it. He was running at full steam and if he had hit her would almost certainly have caused serious injuries, maybe even fatal ones.

Needless to say, two things happened after that close shave. The amorous young bull was sold on to another farmer, and from then on Julie reverted to her original policy of castrating every bull calf born on the farm – without exception.

Julie had acquired a great deal of knowledge through hard-won experience like this. She'd become an expert on raising the young of all manner of animals – even hedgehogs. Hedgehogs were frequent arrivals at the centre. They would be handed in having been found in all sorts of weird and wonderful locations, from cattle grids and garage inspection pits to drains and Guy Fawkes' Night bonfires. Occasionally, an entire litter of them would be entrusted to us.

Julie always did a great job weaning and raising them, but she learned a valuable lesson dealing with one particular brood. She would hand-feed every baby hedgehog and did so with this litter. Unfortunately, she didn't know the hedgehogs were carrying a really virulent skin condition, which she then contracted. It was excruciatingly painful and she eventually lost most of the skin on one of her infected hands. Ever since, she and every other member of staff at the RSPCA centre has taken great care to wear protective gloves when handling seemingly innocent hedgehogs. The lesson had been learned.

Julie's greatest area of expertise, however, was probably in lambing. Each spring now for as long back as I could remember, she had delivered our lambs. Again, she had learned many valuable lessons along the way, none more precious than when we delivered our first batch of lambs in our first spring at Ferndale. We'd bought several Jacob lamb ewes the previous autumn, and two of them had fallen pregnant by a ram we'd borrowed from a local farmer. We were both nervous when lambing time arrived. If all was straightforward, we were confident of being able to deal with it. Our greatest fear was that there would be complications, and of course that's what we got.

One morning Julie noticed that a ewe was having problems. She was straining, obviously ready to produce, but seemingly unable to get things moving. Later we learned that this condition is known as ring birth; the lambs are unable to pass into the birth canal. At the time we didn't know what was wrong.

The vet Julie phoned for help arrived later than promised and with a girlfriend in tow. Apparently keen to impress her with his veterinary skills, he rolled up his sleeves and confidently took charge. 'Nothing to worry about,' he said. 'You just need to know what you are doing. We'll soon have these lambs out.'

He was true to his word, in one respect. The lambs were indeed soon removed from their mother's womb, but all three of them were stillborn. They had all perished, probably minutes before his arrival. He admitted later that if he'd got there an hour earlier the lambs would have been saved.

Ever since then Julie had dedicated herself to learning all she could about delivering lambs. She was driven by a determination that this would never happen to her again. She soon became something of an expert at even the most complex births. On more than one occasion I'd watched in wonder as she'd used her tiny hands to reach inside a ewe's womb to untangle lambs that had become entwined.

On the funnier side of things, our ovine community

had produced their share of characters over the years too, none more entertaining than a little Welsh ewe that arrived at the RSPCA centre and ended up as a part of our private flock. The ewe had been found wandering around the roads near St Agnes, where, it was assumed, she had fallen, unseen by the driver, through the slats of a cattle transporter. She had taken some catching. The inspector who responded to the call spent most of an afternoon chasing the ewe across fields and hedges and a small stream. He'd eventually had to resort to rugby-tackling her and had arrived at the centre smeared and splattered in mud.

The ewe was healthy but extremely wild and we knew immediately that we would have trouble placing her in a new home. Fortunately – or perhaps unfortunately, given the way events unfolded – she solved the problem herself one autumn morning when she jumped over the compound fence and joined Julie's small flock of Jacob sheep in the fields behind the house.

If this was a surprise, it was even more of a shock when she produced a lamb – a male – the following spring. The ram lamb was very small, like its mother, with a similar skittish nature and the same distinctive inward-curling horns. As the 'black sheep' of the flock, the ram was pretty much ignored by Julie. She castrated the other males born to the Jacob flock but left the Welsh ram intact. By the autumn, of course, the ram had grown and had developed the urges normally associated with a healthy male sheep.

One morning we noticed he was missing and started

scouring our land for him. It didn't take us long to find him. A neighbour had just put twenty or so young ewes into a field adjoining ours. The ram had not only let himself in there, he had also proceeded to drive the farmer's three rams away from the ewes and was now enjoying the female company to the hilt.

Julie and I climbed into the field hoping to remove him but he proved just as elusive as his mother. In the end we gave up trying to catch him and trudged off to see the neighbour to break the bad news. Fortunately, he saw the funny side of it. He promised to use his dogs to drive the ram out of the field and return him to us later that day. It wasn't until several weeks later that the ram finally appeared, however, and when he did, he was a shadow of the animal he'd been when he'd left us. He did, however, seem to have a rather large smirk on his face.

A couple of nights after the first calf was produced, Julie and I were back in the lower fields. There wasn't even a moon to guide us, so finding our way was difficult. As we reached the bottom of the fields where they join the woods, we could just about pick out the cow standing in the lee of a hedge and began carefully walking towards her. Suddenly and seemingly out of nowhere, a large dark shape rose from the grass and dashed towards us. Julie and I were glued to the spot for a moment and only managed to dive away from the charging creature with a split second to spare. After missing us by a foot or so the creature continued on and was quickly swallowed up in the gloom.

'What the blazes was that?' I said.

'I don't know. The Beast of Bodmin, perhaps,' Julie said, half laughing.

We were interrupted by the sound of the cow bellowing at the top of her voice. She too was soon visible galloping towards us and then on across the fields in the direction of the woods.

'I haven't a clue what's going on here,' said Julie. 'Let's go inside and get a torch.' Typically, we had not bothered to bring a light with us that night.

It took us a quarter of an hour or so to return to the spot where we'd seen the cow disappear. As we scanned the edge of the woods with the torchbeam, we found her standing contentedly chewing the cud, while alongside her a rather large calf was helping itself to milk from her udder.

'I think we've discovered the identity of our mystery beast,' I said to Julie. 'She must have calved earlier on.'

Julie stood there for a moment shaking her head in disbelief. 'Well, it must have been quick,' she said. 'I only checked her a couple of hours ago and she'd shown no sign of being in labour.'

We moved in a little closer to make sure all had gone well with the delivery. Julie positioned herself behind the cow's rear end to check there was no bleeding or any other hints of an unusual delivery. All looked well, fortunately.

It didn't take an expert to see that the calf had emerged into the world in the rudest of health. It was well above average in size. Standing next to its mother its head almost reached her neck. We could see it was feeding well and there were certainly no worries about its ability to move around freely, as we'd discovered minutes earlier when it had dashed past us.

'I don't think we have to worry too much about this one,' I said to Julie as we headed homeward again, the torchlight picking out a couple of rabbits and an owl in the woodland.

'Shame,' she said. 'I quite fancied a night out tonight.'

CHAPTER TWENTY-TWO

The Shed at the Bottom of the Garden

The two lurchers cowering in a corner in the back of the van were a truly pathetic sight. They were more like skeletons than dogs. Ribs, joints and other bones were poking painfully through their skin, some like spikes ready to pierce the surface at any moment. Their coats were dull, dirty and mottled with bald patches.

Despite the fact their legs had barely any weight to bear, the two animals were so weak that even walking was too much for them. When I helped the inspector delivering the dogs lift them out of the van, they managed only a couple of strides before beginning to wobble like newborn foals. As we half carried them to the small kennel that had been cleared in readiness for their arrival, neither of us said much. We were both too shocked by the dogs' condition.

The pair of greyhound-like dogs had been discovered a few days earlier when the RSPCA had been called out to investigate reports of neglected animals on a remote farm near Padstow, on the north Cornish coast. The inspectors had found the animals tied up under an old pigeon loft. The loft was in a disgusting state, caked in excrement and infested with rats. The two emaciated dogs were so weak from malnutrition they had barely been able to stand. The inspectors had taken them to a nearby vet's surgery, where they had spent a few days attached to saline drips, and the vet had now entrusted them to me to continue their rehabilitation. He reckoned the pair had gone weeks without having eaten or drunk anything. How they were still alive was as much a mystery to him as it was to me.

I had seen some examples of cruelty and neglect in my time, but this was beyond my comprehension. I was just glad that the man responsible had been arrested and charged for his crimes. In a few weeks' time he was due to appear in court on multiple charges of animal cruelty.

After giving the dogs an hour or so to recover from their journey, Karen and I set about taking a closer look at them. Their condition was even more parlous than we'd imagined. The neglect they had suffered had damaged the dogs in just about every possible way. An inspection of their skin revealed they were suffering from advanced mange. It was clear from the rheuminess in their eyes that they had some kind of infection there too. A glance at the vet's notes confirmed this. The notes also mentioned that both dogs had ear infections, and unsurprisingly, the vet had recorded they were suffering from digestive problems, caused by their stomachs remaining empty for so long. I'm sure the list of ailments could have gone on for longer. Where to start? I silently asked myself.

I quickly decided that food and drink were the number-one priority. They needed to get their strength back, and filling their stomachs with some decent nutrients was the key to starting that process. Because of their stomach problems, however, I decided that to begin with we would feed them small regular meals with high quantities of protein and carbohydrate. Their stomachs were very sensitive. If they ate too much too quickly, they could easily add to their myriad digestive problems.

So that evening, as they settled into their new home, we served the pair a meal of cooked rice with white fish and meat. When Karen and I put down the first bowls, the dogs looked at them for a moment or two, as if in disbelief. They then set about them with gusto, emptying the bowls in what seemed like seconds. It was clear their rehabilitation was going to be a very long, slow job, but at least it was under way.

That people were capable of inflicting such terrible cruelty on the creature we refer to as 'man's best friend' was no surprise to me any more. I'd seen more than my share of horrific cases. One of my first jobs when I'd joined the RSPCA as warden had been to accompany a veteran inspector on a call to a farm near Perranporth, where there had been reports of dogs being neglected.

As we'd approached the house and its grounds, I'd been impressed by the general appearance of affluence. There were well-tended lawns and colourful flower beds, and the house looked immaculate. I'd found it hard to believe there could be anything untoward happening and said as much to the inspector. His reply has remained with me ever since. 'Don't be taken in by the front door, son,' the wise old head had muttered. 'Look in the shed at the bottom of the garden.'

Sure enough, in a small shed tucked away at the back of the garden, we found a small, emaciated dog tied up on a rope and cringing in its own filth. Unwanted and unloved, it had simply been left to die, never knowing what crime it had committed to be cast aside in such a callous manner. Ever since, I had kept an open but cynical mind about even the most seemingly respectable dog owners. The philosophy had served me well, particularly in cases involving those who – on the face of it – were professional dog people.

Not long after that first shocking experience, an inspector and I were asked to visit the home of prominent dog breeders. The couple were well known in the canine fraternity and exhibited at major dog shows such as Crufts. They bred and sold toy-breed puppies to wealthy families both at home and abroad. Their business had earned them a comfortable lifestyle and they lived in some luxury in the Cornish countryside near Penzance. Yet when we visited their premises, we found dogs living in the most awful conditions. Again it was the seemingly unimportant outbuildings that revealed their dark secrets. We'd been shown round their main kennels and found nothing out of order. It was when we asked to see inside a dilapidated old caravan in a remote corner of their property that the truth emerged. We found the caravan crammed full of small cages of puppies. The conditions were absolutely appalling, with cages piled up from floor to ceiling and two or more dogs packed into each and every one of them. Sanitary conditions were equally appalling. There were uncleared faeces everywhere, and the caravan stank of stale urine. The couple were prosecuted and many of their dogs were confiscated from their kennels. Their business never recovered.

It was far from a one-off discovery, however. Another prominent owner, known for breeding prize-winning Pekinese dogs, was also found to be keeping dogs in barbaric conditions. I attended this case with the inspector and found the breeder's dogs packed into a large shed with cages stacked from floor to ceiling.

While the younger, show-quality dogs were kept in relative comfort in lower-level cages, the older, or less show-worthy, dogs were accommodated in cramped cages higher up. The occupants of these higher pens appeared listless and had matted coats, which was unsurprising given that they were living in such unsanitary conditions with so little room to exercise.

The RSPCA moved in to deal with the dogs, while the Inspectorate decided whether to bring proceedings against the breeders. As someone with long experience in grooming dogs, I was entrusted with the job of trimming dozens of pairs of overgrown nails and clipping matts from scores of tangled coats. It was far from plain sailing. Many of the dogs were nervous of being handled and seemed unhappy away from the security of their small prisons.

After much deliberation it was decided not to prosecute the breeder in that particular instance. This, however, was conditional on him getting his operation into order before a further inspection a few weeks later. He passed that inspection but the problems soon returned. A year or two later I met a lady who had visited him to buy a Peke puppy. She'd been shocked to see an elderly Pekinese bitch confined in a small dirty cage. She'd been so touched by the elderly dog's plight she'd offered to buy her too and was duly charged forty pounds. The outlay became even greater when she took the old dog to a vet, who prescribed extensive veterinary treatment.

Ever since those early experiences I've advised anyone visiting a breeding kennel to proceed with caution and never to be dazzled by the credentials of the owners. The true story always lies in the shed at the bottom of the garden.

In the days following their arrival the two emaciated lurchers grew steadily in strength. As they became themselves once more and their personalities emerged, we decided to give them names. The staff and I tried out a variety of them before settling in the end, for reasons that now escape me, on Alfie and Blue.

As the days had passed we had learned a little more about them. Their owner had been interviewed more fully by the police and had provided information that had been passed on to us. It turned out that both were lurchers. Alfie was half saluki and Blue half whippet. It had been in the fields, however, that I had discovered the more surprising truth about them. As the health of the dogs improved, I started to take them out into the fields during the evenings and was impressed by their behaviour. It was clear that they'd been trained very well at some stage in their lives. I had only to whistle and both dogs would come to heel immediately.

One evening I was leaning over a gate when I noticed the two dogs standing close by behind me, watching me intently as if waiting for some sort of instruction. I had no idea what was in their minds, so, out of curiosity more than anything else, I clicked my fingers. Both dogs immediately coiled themselves up, then sprang forward, clearing the gate with a single soaring leap. They then stood on the other side as still as statues, looking out across the field, waiting for the next order. Well, I never, I said to myself.

Having worked with many a rabbit-catching lurcher in my youth, I suspected these two had been trained for nocturnal rabbit hunting, or lamping. So the next evening I took Alfie and Blue to a field where we'd been having trouble with the large numbers of rabbits. I shone a flashlight across the grass, immediately picking out not only several rabbits but also a highly indignant fox, which had been intent on stalking the smaller animals from the other side of the field.

There was no question this was a situation they had been trained to deal with because both Alfie and Blue were standing by my side quivering with excitement. They were not going to move until I gave an order, however, so I made a soft hissing noise, which sent the dogs racing down the torchbeam towards the rabbits. Given what they'd been through in the past months, neither dog was as quick or agile as he might have been in his prime, so both arrived just a fraction too late to catch their prey. Instead the rabbits scurried into the shadows, probably straight into the clutches of the fox, who had cleverly repositioned himself in the woods.

That was of no real concern to me, however. The important thing was that I had discovered that Alfie and Blue were fine working dogs and that rehoming them was now going to be a real possibility. The only frustration was that I knew the RSPCA would not let me place them where they really belonged because of a policy prohibiting dogs being placed in working homes, something with which I strongly disagreed and had got into heated arguments about over the years.

A few days later I travelled to Truro for the weekly BBC Radio Cornwall broadcast that the RSPCA used to publicise its work. I tended to alternate with Les, the chief inspector, in appearing on the programme. Amid the usual enquiries about troublesome tortoises and pregnant hamsters, one caller asked about lurchers and their ability to control rabbits.

'It's interesting you should ask that,' I said, 'because I am currently rehabilitating an excellent pair of them.'

At the DJ's prompting, I went on to recount the story of Alfie and Blue and their arrival at the centre. I explained that since I'd discovered their talents, they'd helped keep down our pest population and provided several acceptable meals of rabbit pie. Judging by the reaction of the caller and the DJ, the story seemed to touch something of a nerve. The broadcasts often produced instant results. On more than one occasion people had called in while we were still on air offering to take in abused or unwanted animals that we discussed on the show. The reaction this time wasn't so immediate, and understandably so. As large, athletic dogs, greyhound types have never been particularly popular, although those who own lurchers invariably sing their praises because of their easygoing nature and their ability to live comfortably, often folding themselves up into surprisingly small spaces.

A few weeks after the broadcast, however, a family from Perranporth called at the centre asking to see one of the lurchers 'that had been on the radio'. Having been introduced to the two dogs, they said they were particularly impressed by Alfie and we agreed to let them take him as a household pet. A few weeks after that another family took Blue into their care, again as a nonworking dog. I felt sad about this because I really did feel working dogs should be given the chance to do what comes naturally to them, but at least I could take solace in the fact their lives had taken such a positive turn after the abuse they'd received at the hands of their previous owner.

Thanks to the thoroughness of the RSPCA and the police, the dogs' owner eventually appeared at Truro

Magistrates Court. He pleaded not guilty to harming the dogs, arguing that he no longer had the time to work them properly. His arguments fell on deaf ears, however. Having heard the testimony of the inspector and the expert vets who had examined Alfie and Blue when they had first been rescued, the magistrate took a very dim view of his crime indeed. She chastised him for his inhumane treatment and fined him heavily. More importantly, she also banned him from keeping a dog for ten years.

By far the best punishment, however, was the public humiliation that the case brought the man. Partly, perhaps, because of the small amount of publicity generated when I told Alfie and Blue's story on BBC Radio Cornwall, the case aroused some media interest. For the first time in my knowledge the court allowed the man's name to be published, which it was, along with graphically descriptive stories in the newspapers and on the radio. When I travelled around the county in the days and weeks that followed the case, it seemed that everyone had heard of this man's callous behaviour. It was rare one felt that justice had been served, but in this case, to me at least, it seemed to have been. No animal deserved to be treated in the way Alfie and Blue had been. The man had got his just deserts.

CHAPTER TWENTY-THREE

Heading South

December was barely upon us but there was already a chill in the air. Tonight, with an Arctic weather front driving dense, dark storm clouds across the full moon, the weather forecast was predicting a heavy frost for the morning. As I made my way across the fields to check the animals' straw supplies, I could feel the ground hardening under my feet. Winter was drawing in.

I was in the lower fields near a stand of ash trees, adding some fresh straw to the goats' feeders, when I was distracted by something moving in the air above me. I looked up to see what for all the world looked like a white ghost circling the farm in the night sky. I recognised it immediately. It was, like the worsening weather, an arrival from the frozen North, a Bewick's swan. Most winters saw a few wild swans visiting Cornwall. They are always welcome visitors, as far as I am concerned. They are, to my mind, among the most beautiful and evocative of birds, as wild and as white as the Arctic regions whence they come, and none is more beautiful than the Bewick's. Wild swans such as this Bewick usually fly in family groups or in pairs when migrating, but this one was alone, and obviously desperate to find company and shelter from the impending storm.

My guess was it had seen some of the several mute swans we currently had in the swan compound at the rear of the RSPCA centre and come to investigate. For fully five minutes I watched mesmerised as the swan circled the area, round and round, gradually coming down until its wing tips almost touched the wooden posts surrounding the swan compound. Watching this amazing spectacle unfold, I began willing the bird to land and for a moment or two it seemed certain it was coming in for a final approach, but then for some reason, and at the very last moment, it changed its mind and climbed up into the sky to be quickly swept away by the force of the wind, its brilliant whiteness fading into the inky darkness.

I felt disappointed and slightly concerned for the bird. To be travelling in an unknown area on a night like this was perilous. The good news, I told myself, was that Cornwall is a narrow peninsula and the sea is never very far away. The swan would eventually land on the water and sit the night out on the waves, I felt sure. Well, almost. As the end of the year approached, life at the centre always began to conform to a pattern. Just as the spring and the summer brought their own particular problems, so the colder months of the year tended to bring their familiar faces, the migrating swans among them.

My sighting of the Bewick was not the first swan I'd encountered as autumn gave way to winter, nor would it be the last. Three weeks earlier I had been summoned to the office by shouts from Karen. I'd long since learned to expect the unexpected but the news she had left even me shaking my head.

'Rex, the police need you to get out to the Newquay Road. There's a swan causing a giant traffic jam,' she said breathlessly.

A young cygnet had crashed on to the road a few miles away, picking up what appeared to be quite serious injuries. According to the police, it was flapping around in a distressed state in the middle of the road.

'Apparently, the police are holding everyone back, but they're worried people's patience won't last,' Karen told me.

Fortunately, the location the police had given Karen was relatively easy for me to reach. 'Tell them I'll be there in four minutes,' I said, grabbing some equipment from the storeroom and heading to the van.

Such incidents weren't, in fact, that unusual. Many bird species fly at night, either migrating or simply moving around their territory. Unfortunately, while their internal guidance systems are generally excellent, their eyesight isn't always so good. Many was the occasion when we'd had to rescue birds that had mistaken roads for rivers and streams, usually after heavy rain has made the tarmac's surface glisten and appear like water.

For some reason I'd never fathomed, grebes were the species most prone to being taken in by this optical illusion, and this often led to major problems. Grebes have legs set far back on their bodies and so have great difficulty in walking on land and even greater problems when it comes to taking off from a flat surface. Once they have landed on a road, they are literally grounded. Over the years both great crested and dabchick grebes had been brought to the centre, in most cases by kindly motorists who had seen them stranded on the road and rescued the birds from probable death.

It is easy to shake one's head at the stupidity of animals that make this kind of mistake. Who could possibly mistake dry land for water? Except, of course, humans are capable of making the same error themselves. One of the funniest stories that had done the rounds among RSPCA staff during my time as warden of the centre involved an inspector who was posted to a new district and was just starting his first night shift. The first call he got was to rescue a swan that had apparently been stranded on a frozen lake. The inspector went to the location and spotted the swan, just. It was a dark night and he could barely make out the white shape of the bird standing several yards out on the ice. Having no idea how deep the lake was, he decided to call for backup and contacted the local police. A squad car quickly arrived at the scene and the inspector explained the situation to the constables who'd come to his aid.

'I'm new to the area, so I don't know this stretch of water and don't know how thick the ice is likely to be,' he said. 'For all I know it could be really deep. I didn't want to take the risk without some local knowledge.'

The constable looked at him with a sly smile before calmly informing him that he didn't need to worry. 'I've never heard of anyone drowning in a frozen car park,' he said.

It turned out the call had been made by another inspector who'd seen the swan earlier in the evening and had decided to have a bit of mischievous fun at his new colleague's expense. Apparently the new recruit had turned the icy air blue when he realised what had happened.

Swans also mistake wet and icy roads for lakes or rivers, and this was clearly what had happened in this instance. I arrived to find a police car parked across the road and a policeman holding up the traffic. I saw the swan lying in the middle of the road refusing to move. The information we'd been given seemed accurate. It appeared to be a young cygnet that had sustained damage to one wing.

Contrary to the old wives' tales about swans being dangerous creatures capable of breaking a man's arm with a mere flap of their wings, I'd always found them to be good patients. They were only really aggressive in the breeding season when they were defending their nests and young, with the male cobs being the most protective. This wasn't the case here, so I didn't expect any real trouble, and so it proved. Though in considerable pain, the cygnet didn't react when I approached it. Because of its relatively small size it wasn't difficult to pick up, so I moved in and lifted it over to the grass verge, where I then carefully placed it in the carrying bag. Within minutes of my arrival the police were allowing the traffic flow to return to normal. I thanked the police for their sensible action and headed back to the centre.

There were no vets locally who specialised in birds, so I was forced to examine the swan myself. I saw that the area of the wing that was injured – the human equivalent of the wrist – was badly bruised and swollen. I could also see that some skin had been removed by the rough surface of the road, leaving an open wound, which was full of grit. This would have to be cleaned thoroughly. I did this with warm water and cotton wool, then dried the area with a soft cloth before applying antiseptic powder.

Rather than bandage the damaged wing, I used the bird's good wing as a support. I'd done this before with great success. I taped the long flight feathers of the damaged wing over the flight feathers of the other wing using sticky tape, taking care not to place the adhesive strip too far down the flight feathers. I knew this could potentially tip the bird off balance, so I placed the tape about an inch from their tips. With the damaged wing now held in place in a comfortable, natural position, the cygnet could rest, allowing its injuries to heal.

The bird seemed much less agitated after I'd treated it and settled down for the night comfortably. Within a couple of weeks it would with luck be released on the Fal river to carry on with its life. If all went to plan, it would have learned its lesson and would be more wary of wet roads in future.

*

The crash-landed swan was still in the compound when the Bewick's swan had passed over that wintry night. It was still there a couple of weeks later when we took delivery of another relative, this time a large whooper cygnet. The cygnet had been found by a passer-by who had noticed a bundle of brown and white feathers collapsed in a nearby field. Young wild swans have to be pretty fit to make the epic journey from the frozen North to the warmer climes of the South-west, and the first trip can be too much for some. Clearly it had been beyond this particular bird, which had dropped to earth in the fields nearby from pure exhaustion.

The cygnet was in a pretty poor state, but at least, after a closer examination, I was satisfied it had no bone fractures. I put it on a folded blanket in an indoor pen with an infrared lamp suspended overhead and left it to settle in.

When I returned several hours later, the swan had its head up. It seemed a little stronger and was dabbling in a container of water with grain at the bottom. Although swans are quite capable of picking up grain from the ground, they find it easier to do so when it is placed in water.

By the following morning things were looking even better. The cygnet was walking around the confines of its pen and backing off and hissing at me when I approached. It was clearly time for the swan to move out of intensive care and join the mute swans we had in the compound. It was soon enjoying itself there, swimming on the pond, preening and feeding with the others, but it was clear it was ready to leave. Every so often it would stretch its long neck and point its beak skyward, searching, no doubt, for the family from which it had been separated for the first time in its young life. One morning I saw it desperately trying to fly, running the length of the compound with extended wings.

As each day passed, it became more and more obvious it was time for the swan to leave us, but where to release it? We needed to reunite the swan with some other whoopers, and although it was highly likely there were more of the birds somewhere in Cornwall, I had no idea where they were.

One morning I telephoned the Cornwall Birdwatchers for advice and was told that several whoopers had been seen recently on the Abbey Pool at Tresco, one of the Isles of Scilly. The feeling was that they had now moved off and were possibly back on the mainland somewhere in west Cornwall, a favourite wintering spot.

With Christmas looming, things had got quieter at the centre, so I decided it had to be worth hitting the road in search of these whoopers. I had a good idea of their favourite haunts in the western part of the county.

'Fancy a drive?' I said to Julie, as she appeared from the garden.

'Where to?'

'I don't know,' I said. 'It might be a bit of a magical mystery tour.'

'Go on, then.'

We put the bird in a swan bag, which we placed in the back of the car, and set off. We decided that our best bet was to drive south-west towards Land's End, checking the big reservoirs and estuaries on the way.

Our first port of call was the Hayle estuary, a favourite wintering place for wildfowl. We soon saw that the estuary was populated by large flocks of duck, widgeon, mallard and shelduck, together with many species of waders but no swans, apart from a couple of pairs of mute. Today they had also been joined by huddled groups of birdwatchers, muffled in thick jackets against the biting wind. With no sign of whoopers, we left them to it.

From Hayle, we headed further south to Mount's Bay, near Penzance, but apart from an unidentified grebe and two great northern divers busily fishing for crabs, we again drew a blank. Neither of us was too disappointed, however. As always the magical beauty of the castle on its island held us spellbound. We sat in the car with our binoculars watching the sanderlings and dunlins running along the tideline for what must have been half an hour before realising we had better get a move on if we were going to get this swan launched before dark.

On through Penzance our next port of call was Drift Reservoir, where swans often congregated. Sure enough, a large group of swans were visible in the far distance.

'What do you reckon, any whoopers?' Julie asked, by now getting impatient to release the bird.

I scanned the scene with my binoculars but couldn't see anything other than mutes. 'Sorry, we'll have to press on,' I said.

The countryside was wilder down here in the far west of the county. As we drove on, the landscape was dominated by windswept fields and few trees, apart from where a fold in the land gave at least a little shelter and allowed some bushes and trees to establish, until their tops were forced sideways by the fierce Atlantic gales. It was midway through the afternoon by the time we passed through the village of St Just. We'd slowed down to negotiate the narrow street and were heading back into the country again when Julie spotted a flash of white in a field to the left of the road. 'Stop,' she shouted. 'I reckon I saw a whooper.'

I wasn't so sure. This didn't seem like the sort of place we'd find whoopers, but I should have known better than to doubt Julie. Slamming on the brakes and reversing into a gateway, I looked out into a field in which around twenty whoopers were busily grazing on the rough pasture.

'Hooray! Success at last,' Julie said, clapping happily.

'Don't count your chickens too soon,' I said. 'We've got to get this one out and back together with the flock without scaring them away.'

I took the cygnet, still wrapped in its swan bag, out of the car and walked back down the road to another gateway. It led to a field that was separated from the one in which the swans were grazing by a stone and earth Cornish hedge. Stealth was the key to a successful outcome here, so I walked along the side of the hedge, making sure to keep myself hidden from the whoopers. Crouching low as I went, I eventually came to a gap in the hedge, almost opposite the swans. This was my chance. Carefully unzipping the bag, I took out the swan and placed it in the gap in the hedge. As I had hoped, the young swan immediately saw the grazing whoopers and walked quickly across the field towards them, to be met with a noisy greeting ceremony, strident calls and much head bobbing and wing stretching. There was a chance its parents were somewhere in the group, but in any case the cygnet was back among its own and now stood a good chance of surviving the long winter ahead.

Back in the car, Julie and I poured ourselves a celebratory cup of tea and watched the swans in the gathering gloom. It wasn't long before they were taking noisily to the air and flying in tight formation, with the young cygnet tucked in towards the rear, alongside some older, more experienced heads. Their white silhouettes were soon disappearing into the slate-grey distance, the latest leg of their sojourn in the south under way.

CHAPTER TWENTY-FOUR

Season's Greetings

Christmas morning was a typically enigmatic Cornish winter's day: mild, rather cloudy but with a hint of better weather to come. I was in sole charge of the centre over the next two days. Living next door, it was easy for me to carry out the cleaning and feeding chores and so allow the girls to enjoy time off with their families. I didn't begrudge them the break and, truth be told, rather enjoyed having the place to myself for a couple of days. So I was up and out of the door early, leaving Julie and our visiting family to start preparing the turkey.

It wasn't long before Christmas served up its first surprise. Strolling across the compound towards the office, I saw a cardboard box in the entrance porch. A seasonal gift, perhaps? I doubted it very much, particularly when I saw that the box had a series of holes crudely punched through the cardboard. No, this was far more likely to be the more usual kind of 'present' we got left by visitors. As I'd suspected, when I carried the box into the small kitchen in the centre and carefully opened the sellotape seal with a knife, I discovered a rather aged female cat staring balefully out at me. She was fairly small in size, and her coat was a mixture of white and tabby. She had clearly seen better days – her fur had a moth-eaten look to it.

'Well, happy Christmas to you,' I said, opening the box fully so that she could climb out, then placing a spoonful of tinned cat food on a dish.

The cat responded with a friendly purr and slowly pulled herself over the sides of the box to stretch her legs. She was soon wolfing down the food. The cat wasn't in bad health, as far as I could see, and she was certainly none the worse for being in these strange surroundings. After polishing off her milk, she stretched some more, then padded around the worktops exploring her new environment.

'Better get you off to the cattery,' I said.

The cattery was fairly full, as usual at this time of the year, but there was enough room at the inn for one more visitor. I put her in a cage with a dish of food. She seemed quite at home as I left her to it and headed out to feed and check on the rest of the animals.

I had no idea where the cat had come from, but it didn't take a huge amount of imagination to work out why she was here. The unfortunate creature was simply surplus to someone's Christmas requirements. We had to be grateful for small mercies, though. At least she had been brought here and not abandoned in the countryside or on a rubbish dump, as had happened in the past. The downside of the festive season for us, and indeed every other animal shelter in the country, was the spate of unwanted pets that flooded through our doors at this time of year. Far too often, the season of goodwill to all men didn't extend to our animal companions.

From the very beginning of December the centre would start receiving phone calls on a more or less daily basis from pet owners wanting to dispose of their animals. We'd hear just about every excuse and had heard all of them before. We knew that in most cases the animals concerned were just in the way of the planned arrangements for Christmas. People were acting out of pure selfishness.

The other callers that began to plague us at this time, of course, were people, usually parents, in search of a pretty puppy or a fluffy kitten they could give their son or daughter as a Christmas present. These people were quickly put off. We would explain that, with all the festivities in progress, Christmas was the very worst time to try to settle in a new pet. In any case, in common with most other rescue centres, we didn't operate our rehoming service over the Christmas period.

It was always hard to hold your tongue and be diplomatic with these people, but somehow we managed. Not everyone was so easily deterred, however. And there were always unscrupulous breeders, owners or pet shops out there willing to sell animals to people who were buying them on a whim. After Christmas had passed, we would be left to pick up the pieces. It beggared belief how stupid and short-sighted some people could be.

The previous year, for instance, an elderly lady living in Porthtowan had rung us a couple of days after the holidays asking us to collect the Pekinese puppy she had been given as a Christmas present by her children. The dog had arrived with the family from London on Christmas Eve and had seemed a perfect companion, at least while the lady's children were there to exercise and play with it. But the moment they'd headed off home at the end of the holidays, the lady had quickly realised how completely inappropriate her new companion was. She had crippling arthritis, which prevented her from even bending down to feed the puppy, let alone keeping it groomed or taking it for a walk. She'd been in tears when she rang us to collect her new friend.

By mid-morning I'd done the majority of the routine work. There had been only one emergency phone call: an inspector, asking if he could bring in an injured swan. Otherwise all was quiet.

The inspector arrived with the swan just before midday. As I helped the large bird out of the van, I recognised the bird immediately.

'Hello, Kojak. Come for a Christmas break, have you?'

The inspector looked at me as if I'd been at the festive sherry already. 'What the heck are you talking about, Rex?' he said.

'Oh, yes, this is Kojak. He's a regular here. I'm surprised you haven't seen him before.'

Kojak was a large cob and had first arrived at the centre

a year or so ago in a real state, having been found lying injured beneath overhead power lines in a field. He had almost certainly flown into the lines, scalping himself in the process. He had been brought to us covered in blood, and with skin and feathers hanging in strips from his head. He was a real mess.

It took a lot of careful work to fix him. Once the blood had been sponged from his wounds, it was clear that the skin damage was too severe for sutures to be put in. He would have to remain bald, we concluded. It was at this point that he got his nickname. Kojak made a remarkable recovery nevertheless. After a course of antibiotic injections he was soon fit enough to join the rest of the swans in the compound and proved himself a real character. Within a month or so of arriving with us he was taken back to the mouth of the River Fal, one of our regular release spots.

Kojak was such a distinctive bird and had done so well to recover from his injuries that I think we all felt a sense of loss when he left. It hadn't lasted for long, however. Within a month we had a phone call from a lady in the village of Flushing, set on an inlet of the River Fal. She'd seen a swan with an injured head walking down the main street of the village. The lady said he looked disoriented, almost drunk. He had almost been run over by passing cars a couple of times. When the inspector dispatched to check out the report returned to the centre, we found him carrying a rather dazed-looking Kojak.

He had been a boomerang bird ever since, spending time with us before being released back into the wild, only to be spotted by a member of the public soon afterwards. Part of me wondered whether he'd suffered brain damage as a result of his accident, but another part suspected he rather enjoyed spending a few days on full board at the centre.

He certainly seemed happy today when the inspector and I carried him to the familiar surroundings of the compound, where he joined our other winter visitors. He looked particularly interested in a female mute swan in the corner and soon waddled over to start flirting. He's probably telling her, 'Who loves ya, baby,' in swan, I thought to myself, smiling as I left them to it.

I was just boiling up the kettle to make the inspector and myself a cup of tea when Julie arrived in the office looking worried.

'What's wrong?' I asked her.

'It's Jasmine. She's lying on the ground semiconscious. She looks really sick. I don't know what it is.'

Julie wasn't one to exaggerate, so when she said she was afraid it was something serious I left the inspector to enjoy his tea on his own.

Jasmine was a white Saanen goat with a kind temperament. She was a good milker, but now she lay stretched out on the floor of her pen, her eyes closed, groaning.

'I can't work out what's wrong with her,' Julie said. 'She's ice cold.'

'We'd better warm her up,' I said.

'Well, it's too cold here. We'll have to take her into the house.' Julie shrugged.

'Are you sure? It's Christmas Day. We've got a house full of people.'

'I know, but what's the alternative?' she said.

'I don't know. I suppose you're right.'

Together we carried the goat into the farmhouse. Three of our children were coming over for Christmas dinner, and the first arrivals, Zoe and Klair, were gathered in the kitchen peeling vegetables and chatting away. Having grown up surrounded by animals, they were well used to odd arrivals, but even they looked surprised to see a goat being carried into the crowded house. The look on their mother's face told them it was a serious matter, however. Neither breathed a word of complaint.

We set Jasmine up on a blanket that we lay close to the Aga. I tried not to let on to Julie but I was worried. The goat's temperature was well below normal, and when I returned from the office again an hour later, there was no obvious improvement in her condition.

'I reckon she's eaten something poisonous,' Julie said.

'Where?'

'I had to shoo her back into the paddock yesterday. She was in the back garden. I don't know how she got there. I probably didn't lock the gate properly. Anyhow, I bet she ate something she shouldn't have.'

Heading out to the garden, we quickly found a potential explanation. I had recently cut a privet hedge, leaving a pile of branches and clippings that I'd been intending to stick on a bonfire. They were still damp from the morning's dew but it was clear they had attracted the interest of an animal of some kind. Large parts of the branches had been gnawed at, and many of the leaves had been stripped away.

'If it was Jasmine who ate that lot, it's no wonder she's in a bad way,' I said to Julie. 'Privet berries are really poisonous, and the leaves are almost as bad. You or I'd be pretty sick too if we'd eaten that many.'

We'd made a successful diagnosis, but what on earth was the cure? We had no idea of the sort of treatment to administer to the goat in a situation such as this. I knew the situation was grave and so, even though it was Christmas morning, called one of our vets, Grahame, for some advice.

Grahame was a remarkable man. Now retired, he ran his veterinary practice from a small cottage in a remote corner of the nearby countryside. Locals would drive down the long country lane that led to his door despite the fact his surgery had none of the modern trimmings and he worked without a veterinary nurse. They trusted him implicitly, as I did.

'Sorry to bother you on Christmas Day,' I said, before explaining the situation.

'Don't worry, Rex. I know you wouldn't call if it wasn't serious. I'll be there in five minutes.'

Grahame was as good as his word and was soon knocking on the back door. He took a quick look at Jasmine and shook his head. 'She's pretty far gone, I'm afraid,' he said. 'Privet is pretty lethal if you digest it in the sort of quantities you're talking about. Glycoside is the poison, if I'm right.'

'Yes, that's right,' I mumbled.

'I can give her a multivitamin injection, but I'm not sure it will do much good,' said Grahame.

'Can we give it a try, at least?' Julie said, her face crumbling.

'Worth a shot,' I said, squeezing her hand.

I knew how she felt because I was experiencing the same emotions myself. She was asking herself how she had let Jasmine wander into our garden, always out of bounds to most of our animals. I, on the other hand, was feeling thoroughly wretched at not having disposed of the privet cuttings. Christmas was ruined for us both already, I knew. Julie held Jasmine's head as Grahame administered the jab.

She gave Grahame a plate full of Christmas turkey, which had just come out of the Aga, before he headed off, promising to return later. 'I'll pop back in a few hours to see if it's done any good,' Grahame said. 'Hope you manage to squeeze in a Christmas dinner. That turkey was delicious.'

It was mid-afternoon when Grahame returned to check on Jasmine. Julie had been keeping a close watch over her, hoping against hope that she might revive, but the little goat remained motionless on the kitchen floor, her breathing light and her eyes closed as if she was in a coma of some kind.

'How's she looking?' Grahame asked Julie, as he took off his coat.

'Hard to tell, but I can't say I've seen much of a change in her.'

It didn't take Grahame long to concur. 'No, there's no real change. I'm afraid there's not much more I can do,' he said. 'Sorry.' He promised to call in again later, but didn't hold out much hope there'd be any improvement.

The children knew only too well the ups and downs of keeping pets and farm livestock, but situations like this were always painful, particularly when the animal was almost a member of the family, as Jasmine had been.

'You can't blame yourself for it, Mum,' Zoe said, to nods of agreement from the rest of the table, as we finally tucked into our Christmas turkey, several hours later than planned.

'Goats have been sticking their noses in places they shouldn't stick them for as long as I can remember,' added Klair.

'If anyone's to blame it's me,' I said. 'I should have cleared those clippings away immediately.'

'No,' Julie said. 'You aren't to blame. These things happen. We should know that better than anyone. Come on, let's try and enjoy our dinner.'

An hour or so later we were just clearing away the dinner plates when Grahame reappeared in the back door. 'Evening. Just thought I'd make a final check on her,' he said, heading straight for Jasmine.

This time he examined her for only a few seconds. 'Sorry, Julie,' he said, raising himself to his feet again. 'I think she's slipping away.'

A few minutes later Jasmine breathed her last breath. Julie and I carried her out to the barn, where we left her covered overnight. I would bury her in the fields the following morning.

As we headed back into the house to spend the evening with the family, banks of slate-grey clouds were once more massing to the west. Hard as we tried to lighten the mood, it remained almost as gloomy in the house for the rest of Christmas.

CHAPTER TWENTY-FIVE

Beachcombing

The year was nearing its end, and with Christmas behind us, life at the centre was returning to its normal, relatively quiet routine. The weather had been unusually mild for late December, so the numbers of oiled seabirds admitted had been minimal. At the bird-cleaning unit, we'd treated just a couple of guillemots in the past week. While Karen and Sue had taken advantage of the lull to tidy up the office and reorganise the filing systems, I had started pulling together the figures I needed for the warden's annual report, which I would soon have to start writing.

As I pored over the logbooks and diary entries for the past twelve months, I was taken aback at just how busy we'd been. We'd taken in 1,450 birds, 48 dogs and 505 cats, not to mention of course a horse and a collection of rats and gerbils. Behind almost every one of these admissions lay a story. That was what was so wonderful and endlessly interesting about my life, I thought to myself, not for the first time. I wouldn't have swapped it for anything, no matter how unpredictable it remained.

Darkness was already falling when I looked up to see an RSPCA van drawing up outside. The familiar face of Rob, one of the local inspectors, was soon heading towards the office, waving and smiling at us through the window as he approached.

'Look out,' I said to Karen and Sue, who were buried in a mountain of box files. 'I bet he's after more than a cup of tea.'

Mystic Meg had nothing on me. My suspicions were soon proving well founded.

'Sorry to bother you so late in the day,' Rob said, 'but I've just had a call about a stranded baby seal.'

'Where?' I said, tidying away a file on a shelf.

'Right down at the far end of Perranporth Beach.'

'Below the dunes at the caravan park?'

'That's right.'

'OK. What can we do to help?'

'Well, is there any chance, do you think, that one or two of you could help me go and rescue it?'

'Have you tried the seal sanctuary at Gweek?'

'Yes. They're busy down the coast. Reckon they're full as well.'

'Right. Looks like it's down to us, then.'

I knew immediately that it would have to be me who went. From long experience, I understood that searching for and rescuing seals was no walk in the park. In fact, it was difficult and at times frustrating work. 'I'll go,' I told Sue and Karen.

'You sure?' Karen said.

'Quite sure. You finish off.'

'Can I come?' Sue said. 'I've not done a seal rescue.'

'Anything to get away from filing,' smiled Karen. 'Go on,' she added, with a wave of her hand.

The end of Perranporth Beach that we needed to reach was flanked by towering sand dunes. It was only approachable from inland by a steep climb that was itself only accessible by driving through a caravan camp. If we didn't get there very soon, it would be dark, so leaving Karen to man the phone, Sue, Rob and myself climbed into Rob's van and set out for the beach as fast as we could.

Seals are, of course, a part of the natural scenery here in Cornwall. Colonies of several dozen Atlantic grey seals were dotted all along the coast, mainly between Godrevy and Hell's Mouth, north of the Hayle estuary, on the northern coast. My first encounter with one is still fresh in my memory.

During my early days living in Cornwall, back in the 1950s, I would head out on to the beach at dawn, birdwatching. I would watch the skylarks running through the thick marram grass, the curlew, dunlin and sanderling standing on one leg on the water's edge and the peregrines flying like jet fighters, barely a few feet off the ground, along the expanse of beach. Then, one January morning, as I was walking over the high dunes,

I saw something very different: a large seal lying just at the edge of the surf.

The tide was turning, and small waves were breaking around the seal, so I decided to take a closer look, hoping perhaps to help it return to sea. It was only when I got up close that I realised it was dead. A deep open wound ran from its neck towards its body. It must have got caught up in the propeller of a boat, I guessed. It could only have expired that morning, perhaps within the last hour or so, because the animal's eyes were still intact. They wouldn't be for long, once the gulls and ravens discovered the corpse.

Back then there was no specialist organisation to deal with seals like this. It would probably have been left to the local council to clear the dead seal away. Fortunately, times had changed a great deal. Most of the problems that arose with the seals were now dealt with by a specialist, Ken Jones, who ran a marine centre at Gweek, near the village of Helston.

Ken was a restaurant owner who lived near the beach at St Agnes, just a few miles from our RSPCA centre, and had built his first seal sanctuary in his back garden in the late 1950s, complete with a swimming pool to accommodate the creatures. When he'd started out, very few people had known much about seals, but Ken hadn't been deterred. He'd become a self-taught expert and, thanks to his dedication and hard work, had opened a full-scale seal rescue centre at Gweek that was now world famous. For understandable reasons, most reports of injured or stranded seals now went straight through to him. Of course, he wasn't always able to investigate, and on several occasions I'd gone out either with Ken or on my own. In doing so, I'd learned a lot about the activities of these enigmatic creatures.

Seal mothers are pretty careful about where they leave their pups when they go off to sea to feed, placing them high up on isolated beaches or in the backs of sea caves. However, when the weather turns stormy, even the safest havens can become exposed and waves often wash young pups off, carrying them out to sea. If the pups are over three weeks of age, they have a reasonable chance of fending for themselves, but if they are younger, in the first days of their life, they cannot cope with the sudden immersion in icy water and are left at the mercy of the tides. These pups are often washed up on rocks or beaches far from where their mothers left them, and are extremely unlikely to be found by their parent. In such cases, the cold, shivering and dehydrated pups lie on the beach until – if they are lucky – some beach walker spots them and reports them to the police, the RSPCA or Ken's sanctuary at Gweek. Even when they are spotted like this, it could be the devil's work finding them.

A couple of years ago Ken called one November morning asking me to look for a seal pup that had been spotted washed up on the beach at Chapel Porth. He didn't have time to go himself but told me he would head out there if the seal was in a bad way and needed attention. He wanted me to report back to him.

It was one of those mornings when it seemed like the whole world was grey. On the beach at Chapel Porth, the sky was packed with dense, dark, low-lying clouds, which had merged with the iron-coloured sea so that it was just about impossible to make out the horizon. As if this wasn't bad enough, a strong northerly gale was blowing off the Atlantic, driving in great breakers, which were pounding the shore, sending clouds of spume flying inland like snow.

I'd taken my favourite dog, my collie, Moss, with me. He was often useful in a situation such as this, but not today. Together we walked up and down the beach buffeted by the wind, searching every nook and cranny but to no avail. There was no sign of the pup anywhere. Back at the centre, I left an apologetic message on Ken's answer phone telling him that I had drawn a blank on the beach. Several hours later he called back.

'Don't know what's wrong with you,' he laughed. 'I took a look at Chapel Porth this evening and the first thing I found was a seal pup lying in rocks by the car park.'

I was embarrassed. Moss and I must have walked straight past him. It had been the source of much mickey-taking on Ken's part ever since.

I hoped to fare better today.

It took Rob, Sue and I only a few minutes to reach the beach at Perranporth this evening. At the height of summer the three-mile stretch of sand is packed with thousands of holidaymakers, but today its only occupants were a dozen or so people out walking their dogs before the last of the winter sun went down. Rob drove the van through the caravan park, pulling up as near to the top of the dunes as possible. He and I then collected thick gloves and a large blanket from the back of the van and set off down the steep descent to the beach.

The sand was wet from the ebbing tide, and in the half-light it had taken on a silvery sheen that made it quite difficult to make out objects lying on its surface. Rob, Sue and I paced along the edge of the beach for a few moments before spotting a rather large seal pup a hundred yards or so from the edge of the dunes.

Seals can be difficult to handle, and even the very young pups are extremely heavy if one is trying to carry them any distance. They seem even heavier if they are unwilling to be moved, which was the case with this one. The pup was quite feisty and hard to secure as it twisted its body around, lunging at us with its open mouth. As we tried to manhandle it on to the blanket, it snarled viciously at us. It was a struggle, but after a while we got the pup safely on to the blanket, which we promptly turned into a hammock that we could carry between us. Our troubles were far from over, however.

Climbing back up the face of the dunes, the seal lurched around in the blanket hammock every now and again, throwing us off balance. Picking our way up the steep sand soon became a nightmare, and on more than one occasion Sue, Rob and I lost our footing and dropped down on to our knees. By the time we got back to the van darkness had fallen and we were completely exhausted.

'I'm not the man I used to be,' I said, panting along with the others.

'Neither am I,' said Sue, to chuckles from Rob and myself.

It took one final effort to heave the seal into the rear of the van. As we drove back to the centre, we could hear it thrashing and twisting around in the back.

When we finally made it back, it was pitch dark and the seal had calmed down. It still moved around restlessly, though, as we carried it into the isolation unit, where we placed our ungrateful rescue in an indoor pen with blankets on the floor and an infrared lamp over its head.

Back in the office, I called Gweek just to double-check they were unable to help. When they confirmed they were at full capacity, I called the RSPCA Wildlife Centre at West Hatch, near Taunton, which had a facility for dealing with seals. One of their specialists promised to come to collect the seal first thing the following morning, New Year's Eve. By the time I'd written up a brief report on the evening's activities it was getting late and I was feeling distinctly tired. My shoulder was also feeling stiff after the effort of hauling the seal up the sand dunes.

It appeared the excitement of the rescue had exhausted the seal too. As I made my final, nightly check of the compound, I found it lying peacefully under the lamp, sleeping soundly.

Outside, a strong, gusting wind was building in strength and in the moonlight I could see heavy clouds massing ominously. The weather forecast had talked of the first storms of the New Year being a day or so away. All the signs were that the bird-cleaning unit would soon be back in full swing.

For now, though, all was relatively calm. Apart from the restless clucking of a couple of chickens and the whimpering of a newly arrived dog, the centre was quiet, or at least as quiet as it would ever get. I seized my chance and headed towards home and the smell of something cooking in the kitchen.

More Non-fiction from Headline

AN OTTER ON THE AGA

REX HARPER

**Meet the remarkable Rex Harper,
a real-life Dr Doolittle . . .**

Since opening his first animal sanctuary in the 1950s,
Rex has rescued and rehabilitated more than
50,000 creatures.

In this unforgettable memoir, Rex tells the amazing story
of his life with animals. He describes how, against the odds,
he and his wife Julie built their unique haven in Cornwall.
And how their sanctuary became the county's first,
official, RSPCA animal rescue centre.

You'll meet a menagerie of memorable characters
including Odin the Machiavellian raven, and One Eye
the seemingly indestructible cat. And gain indispensable
advice on caring for every kind of creature, from
Alsatians to zebra finches.

An Otter on the Aga is a story that will warm –
and occasionally break – the hearts of
animal lovers everywhere.

NON-FICTION / MEMOIR 978 0 7553 1628 1

THE HORSES IN MY LIFE

MONTY ROBERTS

The Horses in My Life is a celebration of Monty Roberts'
best-loved horses, chosen from the many thousands he
has worked with over the years. He tells their stories
with great warmth and affection: these are the horses
he has learned from the most, and which have won
a special place in his heart.

Monty was a child riding prodigy. Rebelling against
traditionally accepted methods of 'horse breaking',
he used observation of wild horses to perfect his
understanding of their own communication system
and thus create a partnership with them. With the
support and encouragement of HM The Queen,
he brought his non-violent training techniques
to the attention of a worldwide audience.

All the horses featured have contributed something
unique to Monty's understanding of their kind.
This book is his tribute to their memory.

NON-FICTION / AUTOBIOGRAPHY 978 0 7553 1345 7

Now you can buy any of these other bestselling
non-fiction titles from your bookshop
or *direct from the publisher*.